HIDDEN
HISTORY
of
ASHEVILLE

"I hear tell they've filled a real book with HeardTell posts. A publication you can heft and smell and otherwise enjoy. Whether you use them for research or just plain fun, these columns will surprise and delight. If you are interested in where Asheville and Buncombe County came from, this book's for you."

—Wayne Caldwell, Asheville native, family business owner and author of *Cataloochee* and *Requiem by Fire*

"The bedrock of Asheville is found in its history, and one can easily hear that history at HeardTell. Named for an old and endearing Appalachian colloquialism, HeardTell is a treasure-trove that explores our mountain hollers, cricks and the cosmopolitan city that has long been dubbed the Land of the Sky. That we as citizens and visitors have such a resource available to enhance our understanding of the people and places that came before us is a treasure and true delight."

—Jack W.L. Thomson, executive director, Preservation Society of Asheville and Buncombe County

"Usually it's the historians and writers who seek out the librarians and archivists for information to tell their stories, but what happens when the librarians become the historians and writers? That's what this book is all about. Whether spurred by a puzzling inquiry from a patron or by a recently unearthed rare photo in the collection, the librarians and staff of the North Carolina Room at Pack Memorial Library have used their vast collection of regional books, documents, maps, photos and architectural drawings to tell their own unique stories of Asheville."

—Dale Wayne Slusser, author of *In the Near Loss of Everything: George MacDonald's Son in America* and *The Ravenscroft School in Asheville: A History of the Institution and Its People and Buildings*

"I always look forward to the HeardTell blog posts from Zoe Rhine and the folks at Pack Library's North Carolina Room. As an Asheville archivist, I'm consistently impressed by how they use items from their archives to bring little-known aspects of Asheville's rich and diverse history to light. It's great to see these treasures collected in this volume."

—Gene Hyde, head of D.H. Ramsey Library Special Collections and University Archives, University of North Carolina–Asheville

"Asheville is well known for being a unique town. *Hidden History of Asheville* is full of gems that help us understand how this town became the eclectic place we know and love. It contains wonderful insights and short stories you won't find anywhere else."

—Drew Reisinger, Buncombe County Register of Deeds

HIDDEN
HISTORY
of
ASHEVILLE

Compiled by Zoe Rhine

THE
History
PRESS

Published by The History Press
Charleston, SC
www.historypress.com

Front cover: Peggy Walker Photograph Album, 1908, donated by Chan Gordon. *MS283.001A image 3.*
Back cover: Donated by Lucy Menard of Albany, New York. *MS273 page 006.*

First published 2019

Manufactured in the United States

ISBN 9781467142212

Library of Congress Control Number: 2019935356

This book is dedicated to the Friends of the North Carolina Room for their continued support of the work of the North Carolina Room located in Pack Memorial Library, Buncombe County Libraries.

This book is also dedicated to every single person who has ever donated to the North Carolina Room. We thank you for entrusting your materials with the North Carolina Room.

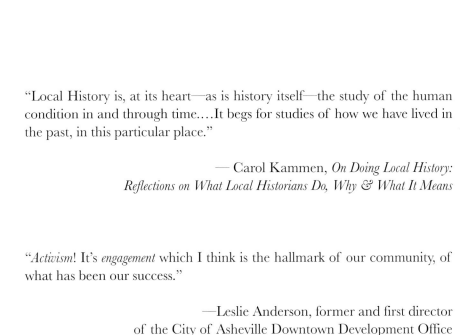

"Local History is, at its heart—as is history itself—the study of the human condition in and through time.…It begs for studies of how we have lived in the past, in this particular place."

— Carol Kammen, *On Doing Local History: Reflections on What Local Historians Do, Why & What It Means*

"*Activism*! It's *engagement* which I think is the hallmark of our community, of what has been our success."

—Leslie Anderson, former and first director of the City of Asheville Downtown Development Office

Contents

CONTENTS

FOREWORD

Asheville has a reputation for being both a little weird and a lot delightful. As the lead archivist for the Western Regional Archives, State Archives of North Carolina, I see thousands of researchers each year. All of them are seeking something of interest, something informative and oftentimes hidden. That's what makes *Hidden History of Asheville* so important. While it is impossible to include every story or solve every mystery (I'm keeping my fingers crossed for more volumes), my colleagues in history have managed to unearth some of the most fascinating and insightful accounts about Asheville for this book. From high-flying history with pilot Robert Morgan or wing walker Uva Shipman to stopping to smell the roses with flower woman Emily Jones, these stories make the past more relevant and give us a better understanding of the community and society of yesteryear.

The mysteries and histories presented here help reveal why this place is so charming and captivating. Where else can you find world-renowned architects like Douglas Ellington and Anthony Lord sharing the same pages with "Big Boy," the world's largest hog? Any place that can boast stunning examples of Art Deco architecture on the same block where a coiffed and powdered hog squealed with delight for "the glory of pigdom and Western North Carolina" definitely sparks some curiosity and wonder!

I've known Zoe Rhine for years and recognize that she has a knack for investigating the past in the most relatable way possible. Without a doubt, these writers have culled countless articles and document boxes, spending copious amounts of time and energy devouring text, scanning images and probing the past to find the best accounts and stories for this volume. The result of all their hard work and research is this rich compilation of diverse, notable and sometimes bizarre glimpses into Asheville's storied past.

The best part is that Zoe and the rest of the writers have done the hard work for us. They've mined these gems of the past from the impressive manuscripts in the Special Collections at Pack Library, polished and curated them into this anthology ready for us to easily enjoy. I am especially grateful for their efforts and continue to learn so much from their work. I know you are going to be as enchanted by *Hidden History of Asheville* as I am.

—Heather South
Lead Archivist
Western Regional Archives

Acknowledgements

The staff of the North Carolina Room is most grateful to a group of 150 people, the Friends of the North Carolina Room. You are our ambassadors. You all are the reason for our work. Your support, financial and otherwise, helps us to do our work better. We're also grateful to the rest of Asheville who just don't know about us yet.

This book contains photographs that, for the most part, have never been published before. How is that? The photographs are recent additions and donations to our collection. Donations are the lifeblood of our collection, and this book would not be what it is without them.

Our HeardTell readers are the greatest, and we are grateful for your interest in the history of Asheville and Buncombe County. Thanks, of course, for all of your *likes* and *shares*.

We are also grateful for the members of the Board of the North Carolina Room, past and present, who give so much of their time and creative energy to support the staff and the work of the North Carolina Room. We thank past board members Peggy Gardner, Michael Reed and David Dry, whose care and interest in the North Carolina Room lives on. Hats are off to our current board members (Roy Harris, Joe Newman, Terry Taylor, Lynne Poirier-Wilson and Tammy Young) for believing we could make a book and especially to those board members who raised their hands to be on the book committee for this project: Nan Chase, Jon Elliston, Louise Maret, Marla Hardee Milling and Janis Wolff. Jon took on the work of compiling Louise and Janis's edits and then took on the gargantuan job of editing the whole text himself. Nan took on the job of final read-through. Louise worked her magic on our introductions and kept reminding me that "it's not worth having a nervous breakdown; just remain cool and enjoy the process." And Joe said "Yes" to several last-minute Joe-I-need-your-help-editing emails. Our brand-new staff member, Katherine Calhoun Cutshall, was just in time to come up with some better chapter titles and held her own on more last-minute editing. Marla, dear Marla, thank you for your patience with us. You've been a great captain.

It is not easy to pull off a book. "It's like building a ship!" I said to our commissioning editor, Kate Jenkins, at Arcadia/The History Press. Kate saved us. While ready to have the work completed, I will miss being able to work with someone who is so capable, energetic, creative, supportive and just so pleasant. I also appreciate the kind assistance of our copyeditor, Hilary Parrish.

The North Carolina Room staff also expresses our appreciation to the newly reinstated Buncombe County Library Board for its thoughtful concern for the library system and its support of the North Carolina Room. The board worked hard to select a new library director, Jim Blanton, who has to be the most creative and qualified director anyone could have wished for. We thank him for his deep interest and admiration for local history rooms, and we look forward to a future with his guidance and support.

INTRODUCTION

E veryone has a story to tell." I first heard this more than thirty years ago from my religion professor, Fred Ohler, at Warren Wilson College, and it has stayed with me ever since. The story of a person's life has always seemed central to my work as a librarian in the North Carolina Room, as this city's past, present and future are made up of the lives of those who live here. We live *here*, in this particular city, at this particular time.

I have always considered it important to search out, find and tell the stories of everyday people who have lived here. So many have contributed so much, with at the most, a passing newspaper story about them at the time, and then they have been forgotten. During one of our Oral History Workshops, one of the participants, co-worker Vance Pollock, said he's always had an interest in getting people's stories because of what someone said to him as a child: "Every time someone dies, it's like a library has been burned."

Every photograph has a story to tell, too. You just have to find it. Buildings have their own stories as well, with a beginning, usually a long history and, sometimes, an end. Communities sometimes, sadly, end as well, usually because of someone's mistaken ideas of "progress." Living in Asheville, we know that inclines, hills and even mountains can sometimes come to sad ends. Objects have stories—objects like a German cannon or a salvaged firebox. And animals, too, have their own stories, like an Asheville pig named Big Boy.

This book is a compilation of stories we've gathered and told in the North Carolina Room blog, HeardTell. Several of these have benefited from further research and expansion since they were first published. HeardTell was born on July 7, 2013, when a library intern, Susan Toole, embarked on her project of helping a public library with a technological advance, such as creating a blog. At the time, I had never read a blog, but I was sure we needed one, so I nabbed her. Susan sat our staff down and, with much patience, helped us create the new blog and taught us what we needed to know to steer the thing.

By then I had researched other local history room blogs and was quite taken by the Brooklyn Public Library Special Collection's blog, Brooklynology. At the time, the staff members of the Brooklyn library were looking for ways to demystify its collection and reach a wider public audience to let them know the collection wasn't just for scholars or professional genealogists. They also saw their blog as a way to reach out to the people in the community who were interested in the city's history. And it was a way for the special collections staff to convey their enthusiasm for their work and the collections under their care. There it was: I had found our blog's mission.

I wanted our new blog to have a name fitting to where it came from—something southern and colloquial. Soon we had an index card with about fifteen possible names on it, including News Bits, News Bites, Bits & Pieces, Intelligencer, You'ns Do'ns, Whimmy Diddle, Listen At, Rattle Trap, Run Ago, A Straddle, Say What…we were getting closer. Then I landed on "Heard Tell." If you hear tell (of) something, someone tells you about it. "Have you heard tell anything new about Asheville history?" It had a nice connection with the oral storytelling tradition.

Five years later, with the Board of the Friends of the North Carolina Room's blessings, we set out to publish our first book. *Hidden History of Asheville* is a compilation of some of our best blog stories. The stories shine a light into a hidden space and reveal something almost gone, including some stories of some of Asheville's residents, streets and buildings, now mostly all forgotten or unknown.

—Zoe Rhine

PART I

STERLING CHARACTERS

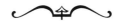

Chapter 1

THE LOST PICTURE

So often pieces of history get tossed in the dumpster. While we're not above diving into such to retrieve items of historical significance, we encourage people to bring us their "old junk" before throwing it away. Recently, a man renovating a house on East Chestnut Street found a box of letters and pictures, stored away years ago and long forgotten, and brought it to the North Carolina Room. In this case, we are grateful to our anonymous donor for this exciting photograph.

> *Remembering speechlessly we seek the great forgotten language, the lost lane-end into heaven, a stone, a leaf, an unfound door. Where? When? O lost, and by the wind grieved, ghost, come back again.*
> —*Thomas Wolfe,* Look Homeward, Angel

The signs on the buildings gave the first clues to unlocking the secrets of the mystery photo. Turn-of-the-century Asheville city directories show the business address of architect and contractor James Albert Tennent at 20 South Court Square. Since Court Square was renamed Pack Square around 1903, we looked further back to the 1896–97 *Asheville City Directory*, which was the first to list W.O. Wolfe's monument shop, along with J.A. Tennent and the office of attorney Harrison B. Brown at the corner of Market Street and Court Square. The Wolfe Building is easily identified in the photograph of South Court Square, taken after the Commerce Building replaced the small building to the right of Tennent's offices. Construction began on the Commerce Building in 1904.

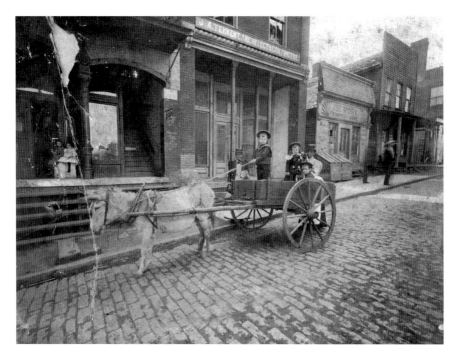

Storefronts on brick-paved Court Square, 1896–1905. *L858-11.*

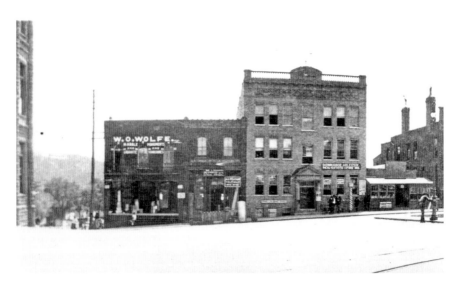

The south side of Pack Square, 1907–8, includes W.O. Wolfe's monument shop visible at left. *F735-8.*

Aside from those discoveries, who are the children in the photograph? Because the location is the Wolfe Building, we looked at photographs of the Wolfe family around the turn of the century. The five children, with two girls sitting on W.O. Wolfe's shop's porch, appear to be about as old as the Wolfe children would have been in 1899.

Our North Carolina Room Collection owns two photographs of members of the Wolfe family as they appeared in 1899, about a year before Thomas Wolfe was born. In one of them, the family is gathered in the yard of 92 Woodfin Street on July 4, 1899. Julia Wolfe waited until her boys started school to cut their hair. In this photo, taken the summer before the twins began school, Grover's hair is short, but Ben and his younger brother Fred still have long curls. Compare the faces of the boys with close-ups of the boys in the wagon.

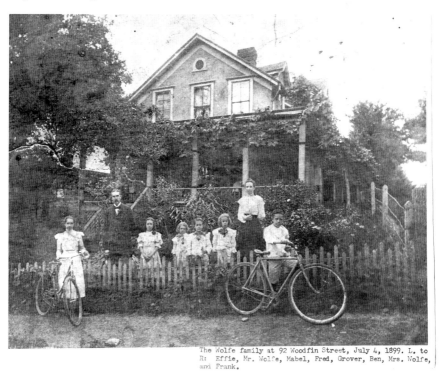

The Wolfe family at 92 Woodfin Street, July 4, 1899. L. to R: Effie, Mr. Wolfe, Mabel, Fred, Grover, Ben, Mrs. Wolfe, and Frank.

The Wolfe family at 92 Woodfin Street, July 4, 1899. *W030-8*.

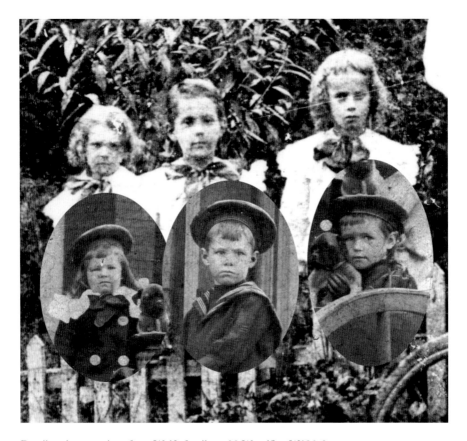

Detail and comparison from Wolfe family at 92 Woodfin. *W030-8.*

The picture above shows the Wolfe twins with their big boy haircuts in the fall of 1899, standing with their class at Orange Street School. Grover and Ben are wearing sailor suits like the boys in the wagon. Again, compare the faces of the boys.

Our mystery donation is a rare, intimate street-level view of the front of the monument shop of Thomas Wolfe's father. The image is also important in that it shows buildings that no longer exist in other photos we have of the site. But is the photograph also a previously unknown portrait of Thomas Wolfe's siblings? Join us in speculation about the identity of the people in the photograph. What are the chances that another group of five children, including a set of twins, of the same ages and sexes as the Wolfe children, would be posing in front of Wolfe's monument shop?

Chapter 2

IN ONE PHOTO, A WINDOW
ON FAMILY HISTORY

T.W. Patton, a Civil War captain and later a mayor of Asheville, built the house now known as the Patton-Parker House at 95 Charlotte Street. Over the years, his granddaughter Mary Parker would sort through material and donate items to the North Carolina Room. She would invite library staff to sit with her on the front porch of her family home, formerly the site of a Civil War encampment. While we sipped wine and she a double finger of Scotch on ice, we'd listen to her funny and surprising stories, none of which was the kind found in the local history books. Her family's donations not only offer rich information regarding the influential Pattons but provide clues to other family histories as well.

L ooking through a stack of photographs we received from the Patton-Parker family after the death of Mary Parker, this one in particular was intriguing, and the writing on the back revealed some unfamiliar names.

The Ravenel family lived at 2 Short Street in Biltmore Village. Short Street became Kitchen Place in the 1931 renaming of streets. Number 2 Kitchen Place is last listed in 1942, but we couldn't find out what happened to the house, whether it was razed or burned. It was gone by 1947 when the Penguin, a frozen custard drive-in, opened there. It would have been on the current site of land opposite where the Wells Fargo Bank stands now.

Who was Samuel Prioleau Ravenel? He was born in South Carolina in 1868, the son of Samuel Prioleau Sr. and Margaretta Ravenel. A lawyer by vocation, he was in Asheville by 1910. He served as vice president of Pack

Memorial Library for many years, as well as mayor of Biltmore Village. It is apparent that the Ravenels were close to the Vanderbilts.

Ravenel's wife, Florence Leftwich Ravenel, is of much interest, having graduated with honors from Bryn Mawr and been awarded a European scholarship with high acclaims in literature. She pursued her studies at the Sorbonne and the University of Zurich and then returned to Bryn Mawr, where she received a doctoral degree in philosophy. She wrote extensively for publications including the *North Carolina Review*. Her articles were gathered into an anthology, *Women and the French Tradition*. A world traveler, she "was greatly loved and admired by all who knew her and missed her when she died in 1923" at the age of fifty-six, according to the Highlands Historical Society.

Florence's sister was Adelia Leftwich, who married Dr. Thomas P. Harrison. They had three children and lived in Raleigh. The little boy on the horse was their son Lewis Wardlaw Harrison, a frequent visitor to the Ravenel home. Wardlaw went on to work for the Bank of Asheville and married Martha Parker, daughter of Haywood and Josie Patton Parker and Mary Parker's sister. Lewis would have been Mary Parker's nephew.

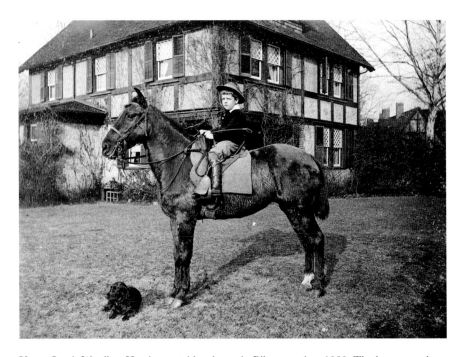

Young Lewis Wardlaw Harrison astride a horse in Biltmore, circa 1920. The house nearby was owned by Samuel Ravenel. *MS195.004A.*

Claire Ravenel, Samuel P.'s sister, was the owner of the horse. Mention of her stay at Carroll's Sanitarium in Asheville when the photograph was taken refers to the newly opened sanitarium, established by Dr. Robert Carroll and later named Highland Hospital. She eventually moved to Philadelphia, where she died in 1951.

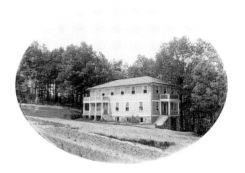

We discovered another point of interest regarding the Ravenel family: several mentions of the family vacationing at their summer home in Highlands. One article noted that their place there "consisted of several thousand acres of virgin forest, surrounding the old Ravenel home, which has been in the family for many years."

The Highlands Historical Society has noted that the Ravenels have almost 180 years of history in the region and contributed "good roads, a church, a popular inn, a public park and Sunset Rock to the town of Highlands," while "later generations were instrumental in saving the Highlands plateau."

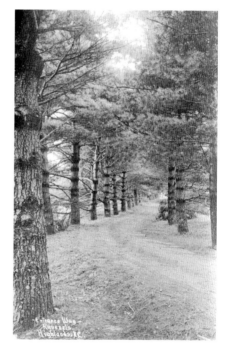

Top: The recently completed Oak Lodge, then Dr. Carroll's sanitarium. It became part of Highland Hospital in 1912. This photo was signed Hage & Koonce, 1909. *G460-11.*

Bottom: Postcard view of the pine avenue leading to the Ravenel home in Highlands, North Carolina. *AA893.*

Chapter 3

GALLATIN ROBERTS: A STOLEN SUIT
AND THE FICKLE FINGER OF FATE

During the Depression, Mayor Gallatin Roberts, along with other public and bank officials, was indicted by a Buncombe County grand jury on charges of conspiring to misuse public funds for the benefit of Asheville's Central Bank and Trust Company. He furiously declared his innocence but committed suicide, leaving behind his wife, Mary, and nine-year-old daughter, Margaret. Margaret grew up in a home of perpetual grieving; her mother kept the house exactly as it was the day her husband died. Many of his papers were locked in a trunk, which no one was allowed to open. The trunk became an albatross that Margaret carried with her until her death in 2013. Her daughter, Linda Burgin, was finally able to look inside and bring the contents—which included photographs, correspondence, diaries, scrapbooks and a key to the city of Asheville—to the North Carolina Room.

With the donation of the Gallatin Roberts Collection in 2014, we received a magnificent story, one as exciting and heartbreaking as any Greek tragedy. Roberts was born under the shadow of a missing father and spent his entire life trying to be the trustworthy, upright man that he wished his father had been. At many of life's crossroads, fate stepped in to determine his direction, and his path seemed to lead ever upward in an irreproachable life of accomplishments and public service. But in the last years of his life, Roberts was brought down by forces beyond his control, and at the age of fifty-one, he ended his own life, abandoning his wife and children just as his father had done.

Often, we can only guess at the details of a person's life, but in Roberts's case, we are fortunate to have a lengthy autobiography that he wrote in

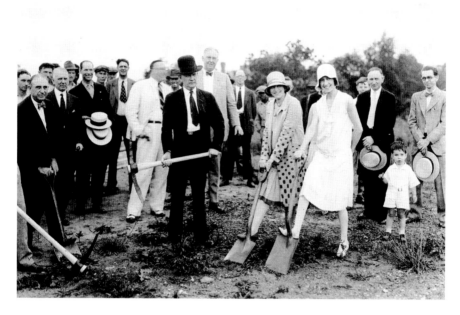

Breaking ground for the new post office, July 1929, with Mayor Gallatin Roberts front and center. *MS255.003CC photo B.*

1927, a few years before his death. In it, he not only describes in detail the happenings and the people of his life but is also very open and eloquent about his feelings regarding his experiences, illustrating the uncanny influence of fate on the course of his life.

He tells how, in the spring of 1895, while planning to enter Weaverville College, he traveled to Asheville in his uncle's wagon to purchase a suit of clothes. After spending his last cent on a new suit at "the old Racket Store," he left his precious package in the wagon and came back to find it stolen. He wrote, "I was a dejected boy. I had no clothes fit to wear away from home and no money to buy any more."

Fortunately, the police caught the thief, and Roberts was summoned to Asheville to testify at the trial. He spent more than a week in court, and "then and there, I had made up my mind that I could do what those men were doing," he decided, determining to become a lawyer. The stolen suit was returned to him, and we likely see him wearing it in the portrait on the next page, taken sometime during his two years at Weaverville College.

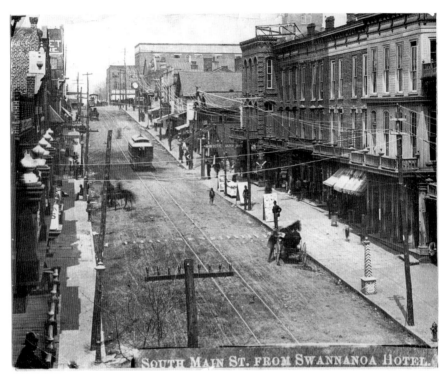

SOUTH MAIN ST. FROM SWANNANOA HOTEL.

Above: South Main Street (later Biltmore Avenue) as it looked around the time of Gallatin Roberts's fateful trip to town. *B521-8.*

Right: Portrait of Gallatin Roberts taken in 1896 when he was nineteen and a student at Weaverville College. In this photo, he wears the recovered suit. *MS255.003B photo A.*

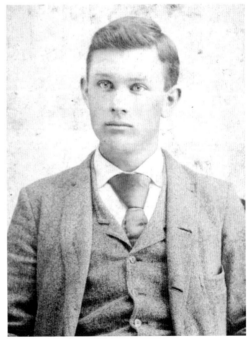

It took nine years for Roberts to achieve his ambition of becoming an attorney. Along the way, he clerked in a store to save money, attended college at different institutions, taught school and finally studied law at Wake Forest University. His profession led to politics—two terms in the state legislature and one as Asheville mayor, a seat he won in 1927.

And so, as fate would have it, Roberts was in office as the Great Depression came crashing down. On November 20, 1930, Asheville's Central Bank and Trust, with more than $4 million worth of city funds on deposit, failed to open its doors, leaving the town effectively bankrupt.

On February 21, 1931, a Buncombe County grand jury indicted Roberts, along with six other public officials and eleven bank officers, on charges of conspiring to misuse public funds for the benefit of the bank. Although he declared his innocence and expressed confidence that he would be acquitted, Roberts couldn't bear the shame of the indictment and the thought of a trial. He committed suicide four days after the indictments came down.

If his suit had not been stolen, would Roberts have chosen a different profession, and would his life have followed a different course? We thank his granddaughter Linda Burgin for bringing us his fascinating story through her donation of the Gallatin Roberts Collection.

Chapter 4

WHO IN THE SAM HILL IS DAN HILL?

Dan Hill has made his presence known, at least to us. His face smiled out of a 1922 photograph from the recently donated Gallatin Roberts Collection. The men in the image (seen opposite, top) were identified by their signatures below their feet.

Gallatin Roberts, the sober man second from the right, was mayor of Asheville in 1922 and in office during the Great Depression when the Central Bank and Trust Company failed, taking with it all of the city's assets. Roberts was indicted in 1931, along with six other public officials, for "conspiring to misapply and convert public funds."

"My soul is sensitive, and it has been wounded unto death," Roberts wrote in a letter "to the people of Asheville" before he shot himself in the washroom of his office in the Legal Building above the failed bank.

But who in the Sam Hill was Dan Hill?

We had never heard his name, but he was determined to make himself remembered. He popped up again soon after in a photograph received from an entirely different source: the Preservation Society of Asheville and Buncombe County.

In one of photographer Herbert Pelton's amazing panoramic photographs, taken in 1923 and seen on pages 34 and 35, the Asheville Kiwanis Club gathered to celebrate Ladies Day on the lawn of the Battery Park Hotel. A brass band made up of club members formed the front row. Dan Hill's boyish, friendly face, with those unmistakable glasses and shock of hair, stood out.

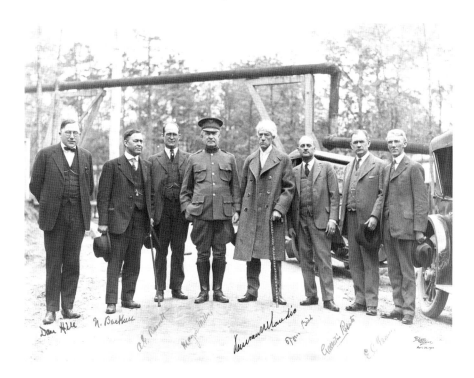

Group portrait of eight men, April 25, 1922. They include Dan Hill, *far left*, who purchased Asheville's first Class B baseball team, and Kennesaw Mountain Landis, *fifth from left*, who served as commissioner of baseball from 1920 to 1944. *MS255.003CC photo A.*

He was drum major for the band and president of the Kiwanis Club at the time. His newspaper obituary records that Dan Hill was Asheville's youngest postmaster, popular with both Republicans and Democrats. "He never met a stranger," the obit noted. He was also an avid baseball fan. In 1924, he purchased Asheville's first professional baseball franchise. When the Asheville team joined the Piedmont Baseball League in 1934, he became president of the league.

But back to the photograph that started the search. With the help of the 1922 *Asheville City Directory*, we were able to decipher all but one of the signatures: that of the white-haired gentleman with the cane. Three of the men, including energetic Dan Hill, were officers in the Asheville Chamber of Commerce. These men in suits (plus the mysterious Major Miller in military uniform) were gathered for some purpose important to the city of Asheville. Pelton always dated his photographs, but even with the exact date (April 25, 1922), we could find no information about this event in our microfilmed

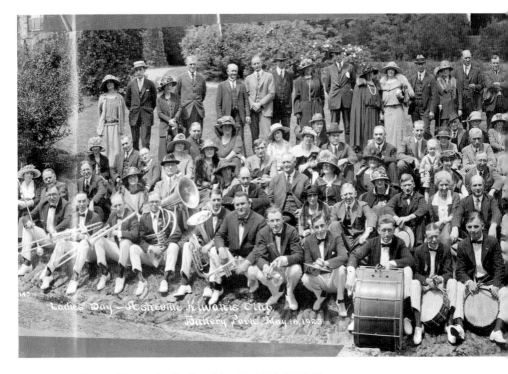

The Kiwanis Club celebrates Ladies Day, May 18, 1923. *F023-X.*

local newspapers. What were these civic leaders up to? Perhaps the answer lay with the man with the cane.

Pondering the picture for weeks, we expected that Dan Hill would speak again if he had anything more to tell us. Enter Phillip Banks, reference librarian at Pack Memorial Library for many years, whose knowledge of local personalities and happenings is unmatched. He glanced at the photograph and immediately identified the man with the cane: Kenesaw Mountain Landis, the country's first commissioner of baseball. After the Black Sox scandal, when members of the Chicago White Sox conspired with gamblers to lose the 1919 World Series, baseball turned to this fierce federal judge to restore public confidence in the game, and he served as commissioner from 1922 until his death in 1944. Our photograph of civic leaders hosting the commissioner of baseball undoubtedly commemorates the beginning of professional baseball in Asheville.

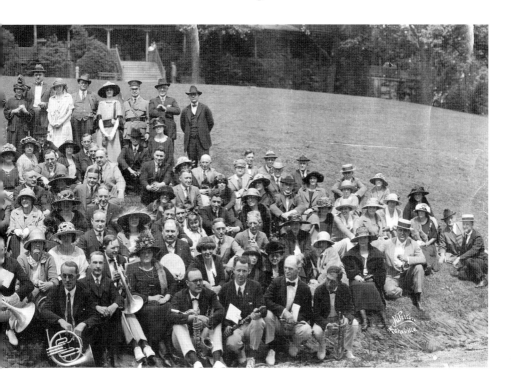

Chapter 5

WESTERN NORTH CAROLINA'S WING WALKER

Pity anyone who tried to keep up with Uva Shipman Minners, who carved a blazing path through 1930s America as an "aviatrix," as she was called in the parlance of the day. Not only was she a pioneering stunt pilot, parachutist and wing walker, but she also raced cars and crashed them with aplomb.

Born Uva (pronounced *you-va*) Shipman in Hendersonville in 1908, this daughter of a reverend was raised in Asheville before setting her sights on points northward and up in the air. In her early twenties, she danced professionally and wed in a self-described "marriage of convenience" to move to New York City, according to her only child, Carol Ann Williams of Hendersonville.

"She always did crazy things," Williams told us in a 2018 interview. She touted her mother's spirit before adding, "I think it was foolishness, myself."

Foolish or not, from the Big Apple, Shipman rose to fame as a dashing daredevil. She dazzled crowds at races and airshows, gracing breathless newspaper accounts that spread around the country and back home to Western North Carolina.

"She was just always different from everybody else," Williams recalled as she went through her mother's disheveled but voluminous scrapbooks—noting that Shipman, a star in her early years, spent most of her latter decades beset by mental illness.

At the peak of her notoriety, Shipman became a popular cigarette company spokesperson. "Camels don't jangle my nerves," she purportedly

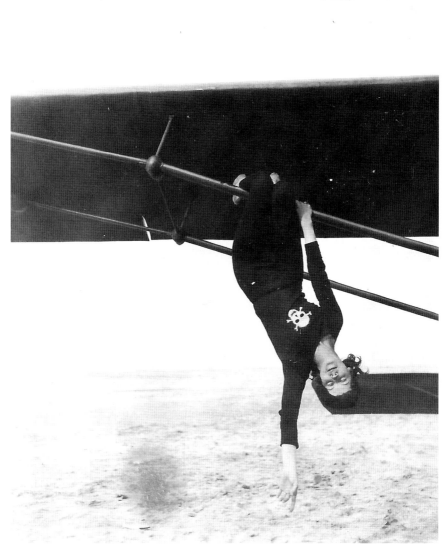

Uva Shipman hanging upside down from under an airplane wing. *Courtesy Carol Ann Shipman.*
O337-DS.

said in one widely circulated ad that touted her parachuting prowess, "and they encourage good digestion in a pleasant way." ("She really wasn't that much of a smoker," Williams remarked. "It was a bunch of hooey.")

Shipman retired from her high-flying adventures by 1940, and after a stint working as a clerk for the Defense Department, she lived at spots around the country before settling back in Hendersonville, where she died in 1997 at age eighty-eight. She is buried in Oakdale Cemetery, where her headstone has an etching of an airplane above the word "Grounded."

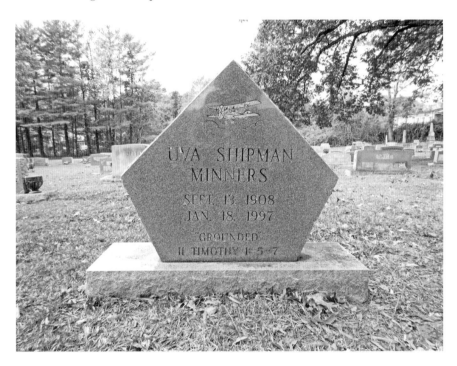

Shipman Minners's grave in Oakdale Cemetery, Hendersonville, North Carolina. *Courtesy Jon Elliston. O347-DS.*

PART II

LOCAL HEROES AND HEROINES

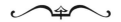

DR. IRMA HENDERSON SMATHERS: FIVE FEET TALL AND ONE HUNDRED POUNDS OF DETERMINATION

Although they served as midwives and healers throughout history, women were nevertheless, with rare exception, banned from entering medical schools until World War I. It is interesting that several early women physicians—including Elizabeth Blackwell, considered to be America's first female doctor—have ties to Asheville. The story of Dr. Irma Henderson Smathers, whose practice greatly impacted the community, is an example of determination and resourcefulness in an era when medical careers for women were still not well accepted.

Irma Henderson was born in Madison County in 1910 to Carlene "Jenny" and Logan Henderson. Growing up in Marshall, Irma painted her dolls with Mercurochrome and did surgery and suturing on their sawdust bodies. She told everyone she was going to be a doctor. They said, "No, dear, you mean you are going to be a nurse." The child corrected them: "No," she insisted, "a doctor."

As fortune would have it, Dr. J.N. Moore, a family doctor in Marshall, boarded with Irma's parents. She idolized the man and accompanied him on house calls. At the time, though, he did not encourage her to become a physician, insisting the work was too hard for a woman and the hours too long.

Irma's parents moved from Marshall to Buncombe County, and after she graduated from Woodfin High School, Irma entered Mars Hill College. Dr. Moore agreed to pay her tuition through college and medical school if she could earn her own room and board. She made her own clothes, taught piano and became a student teacher. Graduating first in her class, she went

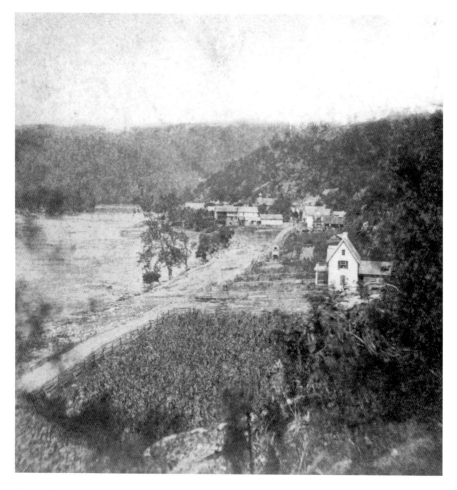

Above: Marshall, North Carolina, on the French Broad River, right before the turn of the century. *D292-5*.

Opposite: Dr. Irma Smathers on the right with an unidentified woman. *MS095.001*.

on to the University of North Carolina at Chapel Hill and from there to Tulane University's School of Medicine. As a medical student, she wrote "bad" fiction under another name to support herself. She graduated in 1933, one of five female students in a class of one hundred and the youngest medical school graduate in the South that year. Dr. Henderson was five feet tall and weighed one hundred pounds.

Irma arrived in Asheville in June 1933, a month too late to take her state board examination. With Asheville still in the midst of the Great Depression,

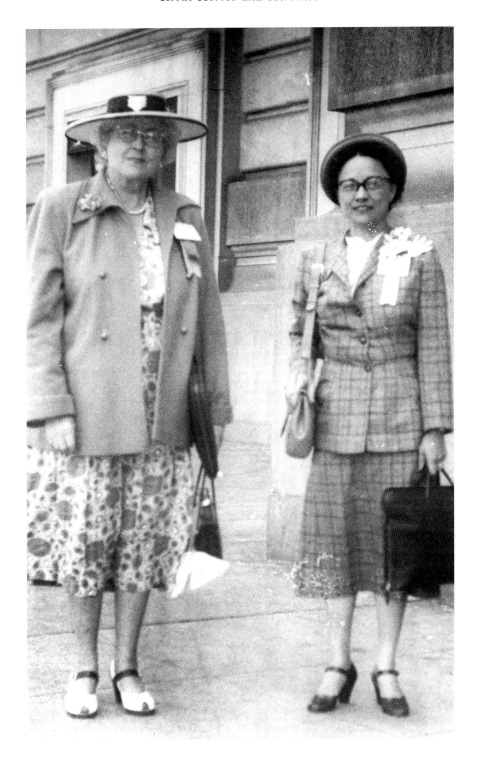

she worked for a year, without salary, at the Aston Park Hospital. In 1934, she opened her general medicine office in the New Medical Building on Market Street, accepting only women and children as patients. She had the distinction of being the first native Western North Carolina woman to practice in Asheville.

The federal government was opening a cannery in Asheville, employing about one thousand people to preserve food to give to the hungry. Dr. Margery Lord, a city health officer, saw to it that new doctors received contracts to medically examine, at seventy-five cents each, the people hired for the cannery. Irma examined all 750 women workers. "I was paid all in one check and it was about my biggest check ever—or for a long time," she would recall. "I paid my office rent with it, put some down on a car, some down on instruments. It just helped, that's all."

After she settled into her own office, she needed, like all physicians, some medical malpractice insurance. William E. Smathers of Autry-Smathers Insurance Agency sold her coverage, and they married the following year. She liked to say of her malpractice policy and her insurance agent, "I've had them for forty years and been very well satisfied with both."

To make house calls, the doctor drove a 1934 Chevrolet that she was proud to say she "could drive down creek beds and between trees." She charged one dollar per visit and would deliver a baby at home for twenty-five dollars. She loved delivering babies, finding it more dramatic than surgery. All told, she delivered more than six thousand, with a personal record of eight in twenty-four hours during World War II. She worked diligently to provide healthcare for those who didn't have their own private physician.

Irma became ill in 1952 and closed her office after twenty-five years of private practice, but two years later, she entered the public health field as a school doctor. When the city and county offices joined, she became director of the city and county school health services. She worked on boards and committees of various local and state organizations, all concerned with public health and safety. She retired in 1975, having been a staff member at Aston Park Hospital, Memorial Mission Hospital and St. Joseph's Hospital, where she was the first woman appointed chief of staff in an Asheville hospital. In a 1986 interview, she said that while there had been improvements in local public health, her main concern was still "the big gap between those who have and those who have not." Dr. Smathers died in 1996 at the age of eighty-five.

In 2009, when Pack Memorial Library was preparing for a renovation, the North Carolina Room staff was making a clean sweep of the basement

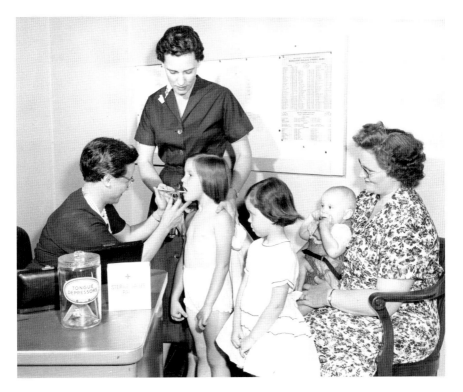

Dr. Irma Smathers, *seated*, and public health nurse Mrs. Ruth Martin examining Rena Jeannette Carland, six years old, who is accompanied by her sister, Ruby Fay, and her mother, Mrs. Lorene W. Carland, who is holding baby Jean, 1958. *N521-8 from the Irma Smathers Collection MS095.*

area where non-archived collections were stored. We discovered a stack of some eighty-five photographs of babies in glass frames. Some of the photos were addressed "To my doctor" and followed by the name of the child. If you were born in Asheville during the 1940s and Dr. Smathers was your mother's physician, we might have your baby picture.

Chapter 7

E.W. PEARSON'S REMARKABLE RUN

A discovery by Pearson's grandson Clifford Cotton II inspired us to write about E.W. Pearson. While cleaning off his porch, Clifford found four letters, somehow preserved in the "trash" there, that provided exciting new information about his grandfather and his mother, Annette.

Edward W. Pearson Sr. was one of the most energetic and creative forces for change that Asheville has ever known. From his arrival in Asheville in 1906 until his death in 1946, he worked tirelessly to improve the fortunes and the quality of life of his family and his community. Facing many barriers to advancement in a strictly segregated society, he saw not obstacles but opportunities.

Pearson, a decorated veteran of the Spanish-American War, had left school after fourth grade but took advantage of every opportunity to learn. He took correspondence courses in insurance, business, religion and law. A savvy businessman, he operated a general store in front of his West Asheville home.

This photo of the exterior of the store shows it emblazoned with symbols of the fraternal organizations to which Pearson belonged. He was a networker long before the term became fashionable, belonging to the Masons (a Grand Master), the Odd Fellows and the Knights of Pythias. He organized and was the first president of the Asheville branch of the NAACP. He also organized the Mountain City Mutual Insurance Company and ran Piedmont Shoe Company, a mail-order business.

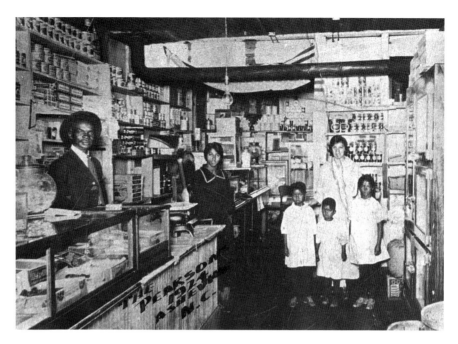

This 1924 photograph shows the interior of Pearson's store and, on the right, the family to whom he was devoted: *from left to right*, daughter Iola Pearson Byers, son Edward W. Pearson Jr., wife Annis Bradshaw Pearson and daughter Annette Pearson Cotton. *L925-DS photo A.*

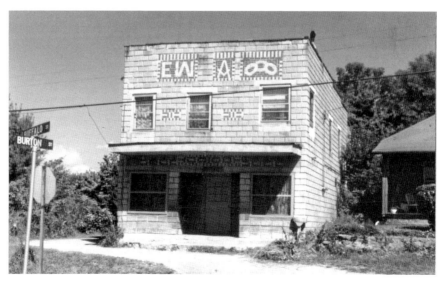

The grocery store of Edward W. Pearson Sr. that was built in front of his home at 3 Buffalo Street in West Asheville. His son E.W. Pearson Jr. ran a music club called the Blue Note Casino at that address after his father died. *L925-DS photo B.*

Pearson also sold real estate, working as an agent for R.P. Hayes, son of the nineteenth U.S. president, who lived briefly in Asheville. Black residents of Asheville were eager to buy lots in Park View, Pearson's subdivision for blacks in West Asheville. A plat map shows the names of property owners—a who's who of black Asheville—from Dr. William G. Torrence, who opened Asheville's first black hospital, to men and women listed as cooks and laborers in the 1915 *Asheville City Directory*.

Pearson's own property in Park View included land he designated Pearson Park. There, in 1914, he organized the first Buncombe County District Colored Agricultural Fair. Held annually for many years, this fair brought black residents from all over Western North Carolina to enjoy amusement park rides and games and compete for cash prizes in many categories, from baked goods to flower arrangement. Here we see Pearson and his older daughter, Annette, at the fair in 1945. The last one was held in 1947, the year after Pearson's death.

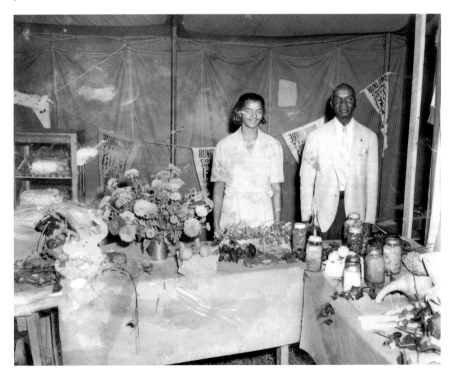

E.W. Pearson standing beside his daughter Annette behind an exhibit table holding canned goods, gourds and flower arrangements at the 1945 Buncombe County District Agricultural Fair. *L932-DS.*

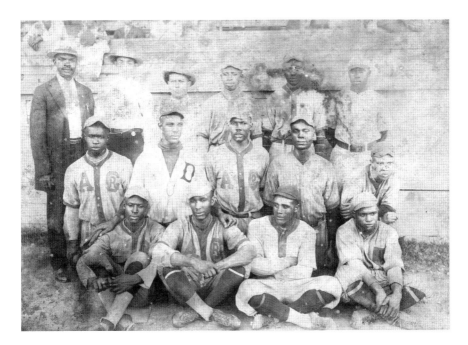

Portrait of the Royal Giants, Asheville's first black baseball team, 1917–21. *B320-5.*

Because Pearson could not attend white-only ballgames in the days of segregation, he organized Asheville's first black semi-professional baseball team, the Royal Giants. At Pearson Park and later at Oates Park on Southside, the Royal Giants played against other black teams from surrounding states.

The letters Mr. Cotton found on his porch were from 1935, when the Great Depression was subsiding but money was still scarce. At that time, Pearson could not afford the tuition for Annette's second year at the North Carolina College for Negroes (now North Carolina Central University), the nation's first state-supported liberal arts college for black students. The four letters between Pearson and college president James E. Shepard describe the creative solution the two men figured out for financing Annette's further education: Pearson deeded fifty acres of land to the college to be held as security until he was able to pay the tuition.

We've been honored to share parts of his incredible life, but given Pearson's many accomplishments, we wonder: is there someone out there prepared to write a biography about this inspiring man?

Chapter 8

TEMPIE AVERY: FROM SLAVERY TO COMMUNITY BEDROCK

Many old photos come to us without full or accurate identification, and it's exciting when we can match names and faces. This 1897 portrait was loaned to us by the granddaughter of Pauline Moore Bourne (who was three months old in this photo) along with the information that Pauline remembered her nurse, with affection, as "Mammy Turpie."

We displayed the photograph in an exhibit with a caption that the nurse was referred to by the family as "Mammy Turpie." A patron who had researched a former Asheville slave named Tempie Avery saw the exhibit and wondered if Mammy Turpie might possibly be a baby's pronunciation of "Tempie." We got in touch with a woman who had previously come from Washington, D.C., to research her ancestor Tempie in our collection and sent her a copy of the photo.

She responded, "I have that same original photo in my mother's trunk. I never thought there would be another family with the same photo. It's Tempie!"

We then put Tempie's descendant in touch with the woman who had loaned us the photograph. After more than one hundred years, it was incredible to think of a descendent of a former slave talking with the descendent of a wealthy family whose children were loved and cared for by that same woman. They had a long conversation that was meaningful to both of them. And just as important, we finally had a face to go with the name Tempie Avery.

Tempie Avery was a young slave purchased in Charleston in 1840 by Nicholas Woodfin. During her time on his Asheville plantation, she became a respected midwife, delivering both black and white babies.

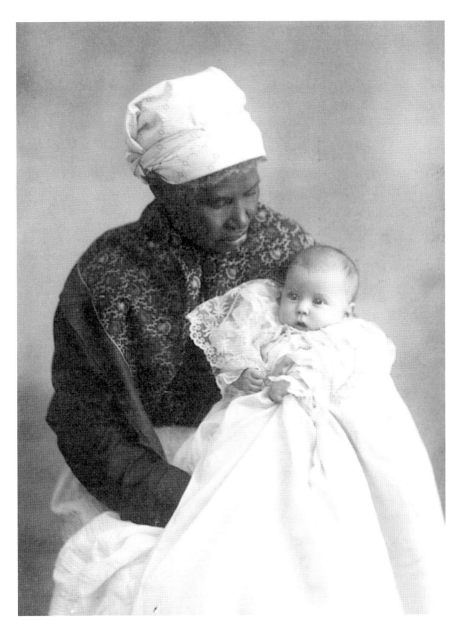

Studio portrait of Tempie Avery in a turban holding a baby in a white christening dress, 1897. The three-month-old baby is Pauline Moore. Her nurse was known by the family as Mammy Turpie. *K949-5.*

Tempie was close to all of the Woodfin sisters but was especially close to Anna Woodfin. Nicholas Woodfin owned all of the land that became Stumptown. In 1868, Woodfin conveyed an acre of land to his daughters to be held for Avery's use. This lot, now 34 Pearson Drive, is the land on which the Montford Community Center currently stands. Anna had a head for business, and she sold many of the original lots in Stumptown.

This map shows that the conveyance from the Woodfins to Avery predates construction in Montford beyond West Chestnut Street. The Stumptown community, most of which is shown in the map in the triangle, was developed on land adjacent to Avery's home. Stumptown was a thriving, predominantly African American neighborhood before the development of the Montford community beyond West Chestnut Street, which began around 1891. As an old woman, Tempie Avery could stand in her yard and watch the neighborhood of Montford growing to the east of her and the community of Stumptown coming to life behind her house to the west.

While Stumptown was less than three hundred acres, it was home to over 250 families. The urban renewal of the 1970s cleared the entire area. By gaining property through eminent domain, the City of Asheville "replaced dilapidated houses and an intact neighborhood with a ball field, a community center and tennis courts," Pat Fitzpatrick, a local historian, would record. "Welfare Baptist Church remains." After Fitzpatrick wrote the article, the

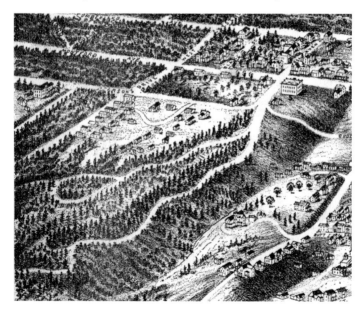

Detail from "1891 Bird's-Eye View of the City of Asheville," Ruger and Stoner, 1891. *MAP202.*

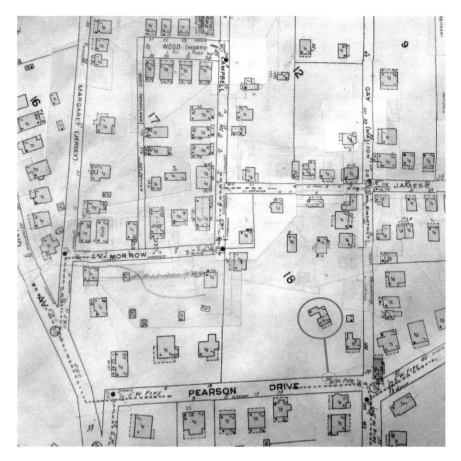

Tempie's home is circled here, showing its shape and position. *Detail from vol. 1, page 55, 1925 Sanborn Insurance Map.*

Welfare Baptist Church is no longer a house of worship. The church closed and sold its property to someone who turned it into a residence.

While Avery's life after emancipation was not easy, she used her learned skills as a nurse and midwife to support herself and her children. A widow before 1900, she also worked as a laundress. According to her obituary in the *Asheville Citizen*, she was a "well-known and respected community member in both black and white communities."

On October 3, 2017, Asheville City Council voted unanimously to rename the Montford community center the Tempie Avery Montford Center.

Chapter 9

G.O. Shepherd Sr.: A Far-Reaching Community Voice

You may not have heard of G.O. Shepherd; he was not a politician or founding father of Asheville. Nevertheless, he was an influential piece of Asheville's history. Over the course of his long life, he took part in every aspect of civic life, including playing a key role in Asheville's first radio station. The collection of his memorabilia, donated by his son, G.O. Shepherd Jr., reveals a man with a keen interest in many things and a dedication to bringing modern technology and communication to Asheville.

Gaylord Oscar Shepherd Sr. settled in Asheville in 1919. At the age of twenty-four, his arrival was well timed, as the city was beginning a decade of rapid growth and was ripe for the energies of a young man with ambition. Through hard work he became, according to the *Asheville Citizen*, "one of the leading advertising agents in the state." Yet advertising was only one area in which he excelled. Photographs donated to the North Carolina Room Collection by his son, G.O. Shepherd Jr., testify to this. In his roles as a business promoter, advertising executive, editor, publisher, radio station owner and leader of the Civitan Club, it appears Shepherd was involved in most aspects of Asheville civic life over the next thirty-three years.

Shepherd's office, a stone structure that was torn down around 1997, stood at the Biltmore Avenue entrance to the Kenilworth neighborhood. The Kenilworth Inn, built in 1917, and the Fontainebleau development on Lake Kenilworth were two of his concerns.

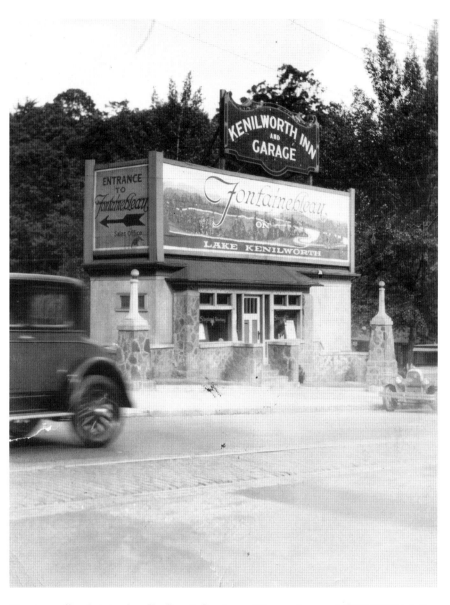

The stone office that stood on Kenilworth Road near Biltmore Avenue. *MS282.001F photo G.*

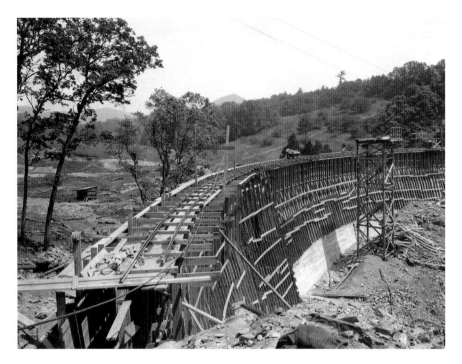

The Kenilworth Lake dam under construction, 1926. Wooden scaffolding supports the structure while workmen perch on top, one pushing a car on rails. *MS282.001E photo H.*

Shepherd became a skilled photographer, which surely contributed to his success in advertising. The photograph above documents the construction of the Kenilworth Lake dam, circa 1925. Once the dam was completed, Kenilworth Lake began to fill. Lake Kenilworth, fed by the waters of Ross Creek, cost nearly $100,000 and provided this "pioneer Asheville suburb" with just what it needed to be a perfect place to build a home.

Shepherd performed as an amateur musician. The photo on the top of the facing page of the Asheville Business Club's Saxophone Band shows him standing on the far left holding the bass sax, 1924–25.

Asheville's first radio station, ABC, originated in a back room of the Asheville Battery Company, which was located at 19 Haywood Street in 1923. Drawn to this new medium, Shepherd joined the station, which soon became WABC. He produced a weekly program called *GOSH and the Gang* that was directed toward shut-ins but attracted a general audience as well. In 1927, the Asheville Chamber of Commerce took over the station's license and changed its name to WWNC: "Wonderful Western North Carolina."

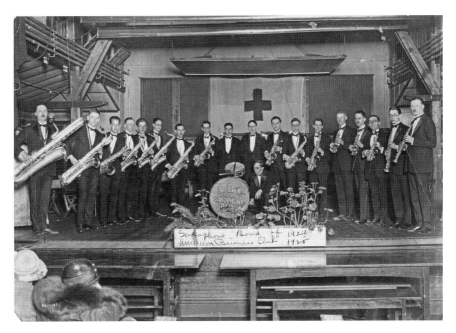

Members of the American Business Club Saxophone Band prepare to play in Oteen, 1924–25. G.O. Shepherd is at far left. *MS282.001C photo C.*

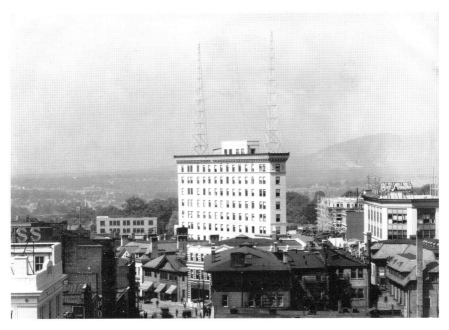

Photo of the Flatiron Building, home of WWNC, with two radio towers mounted on the roof. It includes a rooftop view of downtown Asheville, looking west down College Street. *MS282.001G photo A.*

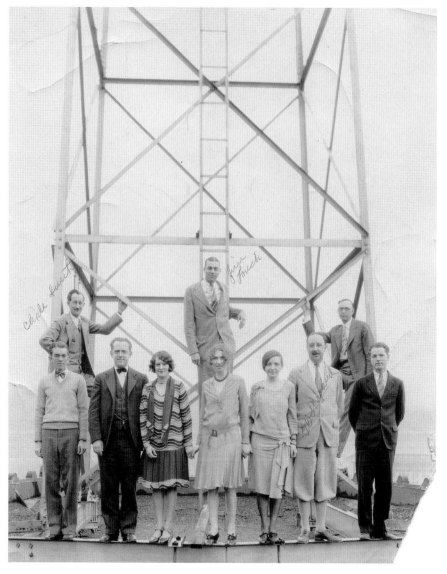

The staff of radio station WWNC stands on the base of a radio tower on top of the Flatiron Building, 1930. *MS282.001G photo K.*

Shepherd managed the station for the chamber before acquiring the license himself in August 1928. Four months later, he sold it to the *Asheville Citizen*, but he stayed on as station director until 1934. "My interest was in listening," he later wrote, explaining that he hired others to work on the technical side. He created programs by writing scripts, hosting musicians

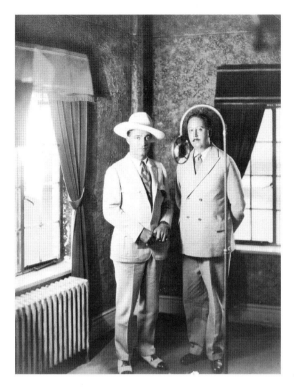

Tom Mix and G.O. Shepherd at WWNC radio stand before a studio microphone, 1930. G.O. Shepherd Jr. reported that the cowboy actor rode his horse into the Flatiron Building. *MS282.001G, photo C.*

and eventually contracting with the Columbia Broadcasting System. During this time, he also wrote a daily column, "Down the Airway," promoting the station's programming. It evolved to become a daily feature in the *Asheville Citizen*, expanding to a full page on Sundays.

The movie *The Conquest of Canaan* was filmed in Asheville in 1921. As an amateur actor, Shepherd must have been keenly interested in the filming as he watched, camera ready. A number of his shots picture lead actor Thomas Meighan with unidentified extras. Shops line North Pack Square, and the 1892 Asheville City Hall and Fire Department set the background for many photos. View these photos at MS282.001l.

In 1952, Shepherd and his wife, Emie, moved to Sarasota, Florida, to live near their daughter, Clare. He lived there until his death in 1963 at age sixty-eight.

Chapter 10

Flower Ladies of
Southern Appalachia

Quite a while back, I ran across a periodical in our book collection titled Our Town *from 1974. The front cover had a colored photograph of Emily Jones bending over large bunches of cut flowers with the dome of the Asheville First Baptist Church blurred out in the background. I remembered Emily, older than in the picture, when she used to stand in the entrance way to JCPenney department store on Battery Park. I smiled to see her face, now long gone from downtown. I set the magazine on my desk, propped up, to remind me to scan the cover to add to our photograph collection. Truly, about a year later, I dealt with her. While scanning the picture, it occurred to me that I should write a blog post about her. So I did. A week or two later, Michael Reid, a former board member of the Friends of the North Carolina Room, and an avid collector for us, came in, smiling while handing me two photographs. The blog post had reminded him of two photos he had purchased several years ago. Flower ladies are pretty much a thing of the past. I like to think about how much they gave to the city, and I agree with the editorial that a monument to flower ladies would be in order.*

The mountains of Western North Carolina are known for their many species of native wildflowers all spring, summer and fall. It is not hard to imagine that women have been gathering wildflowers for decades as a way to make ends meet—just don't expect to find much written about them.

It's a hard way to make a living, to be sure, and most women who engaged in the flower trade didn't expect their children to follow suit. It is too much work. Whether the flowers are picked by hand from the mountainsides, grown in their own gardens or even, as in more recent times, purchased

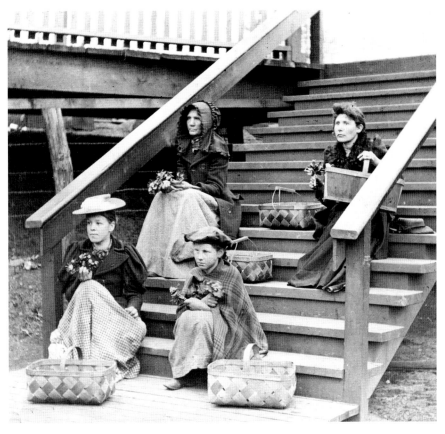

Original glass plate titled "Flower girls at Hot Springs NC." The town was called Warm Springs until 1886. *F896-8.*

from a truck vendor, a woman would have to stay up late or get up very early for the flowers to be fresh enough to peddle. And, after all, how much could a spray of flowers bring?

Still, Asheville residents provided consistent demand for fresh flowers sold by local women.

One resident wrote to the *Asheville Citizen-Times* as recently as 2015, seeking to track down an older woman she was so fond of who had been selling flowers on the streets of West Asheville. The newspaper found the woman's son, Jason, who said his mother, Greta Haywood, was still alive and well but had moved from her house off Sand Hill Road into a retirement home. He said that his mother was a "little piece of sunlight" through the neighborhood for many years and that she made "walking around" money with her sales.

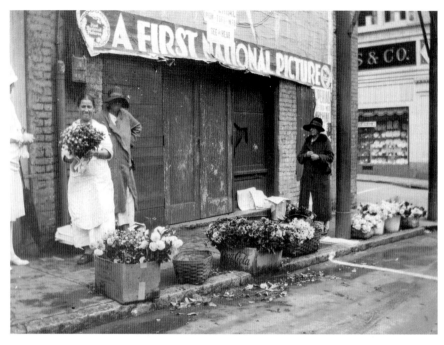

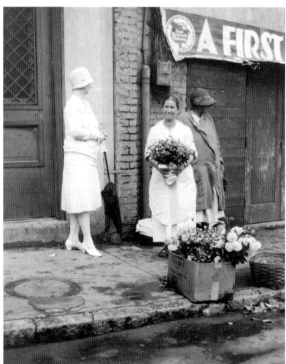

Above: Flower women at the corner of College Street and Lexington Avenue, circa 1930. Welfare advocate Mrs. Florence B. Bynum stands at left. *MS342.004 item 7, photo 1.*

Left: Asheville resident Mrs. Florence Bynum. She was active in public welfare and civic affairs; it is likely that her concerns included the welfare of the flower sellers. *MS342.004 item 7, photo 2.*

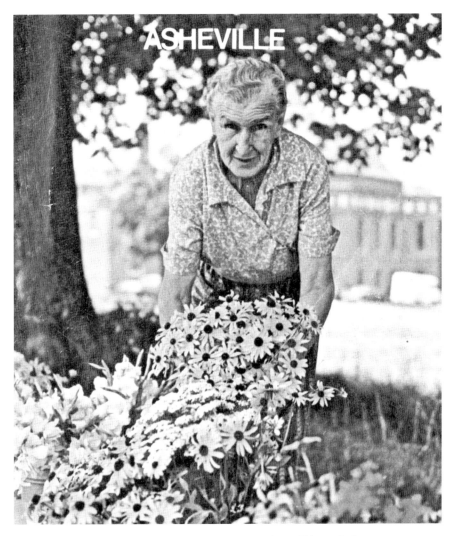

Emily Racy Tabor Jones, age seventy-eight, in a 1974 photo. Tabor sells flowers on Charlotte Street. The First Baptist Church of Asheville can be seen in the background. *0291-DS.*

Emily Racy Tabor Jones was probably the most well-known and written-about flower lady of Asheville, and perhaps the last. Jones was born in Asheville in 1893 to Larkin and Fannie Tabor. She married Manley Eugene Jones in 1921 at the age of twenty-eight. They used to sell wood and kindling until gas and electric stoves came along. Her husband died in 1964.

Jones did not attend school, nor could she read or write. She began her trade on the Saturday before Mother's Day in 1925. Working on the assumption that "everybody likes flowers," she made it on her own selling flowers for almost sixty years on Charlotte Street in front of the former Ingles grocery store. That was back when Mission Hospital stood on the corner of Charlotte and Woodfin Streets. She sold from the sidewalk beside the hospital.

Bob Terrell wrote about Jones in 1970. She sold flowers seven days a week (but not until after 2:00 p.m. on Sundays). "People come from 'fur and nigh' to buy from me," she told him. "They come from Canton, Old Fort, Burnsville, all around." Gladiolas were her favorite flower.

Jones had many friends and regular customers, including Fred Wolfe, the brother of the famous Asheville author Thomas Wolfe, who came by on Fridays to buy flowers to put on his family members' graves. She was quite fond of former mayor Gene Ochsenreiter. At one time, he owned property nearby and rented it to someone for a car lot—and the man told Jones she had to leave. However, "Ochsenreiter told them to rope me off a place and let me be or they'd have to leave," she recalled.

Jones later sold her flowers at the entrance to JCPenney department store on Battery Park Avenue. At one point, florists complained, and the police had to tell her that she was in violation of a city ordinance against peddling. An officer was put in charge of finding her a new place to sell. "I've always tried to work," she told the policeman. "I don't want people to keep me up." Then, the manager of JCPenney came to the rescue and said she could continue her business in the store's vestibule. It was a better spot anyway, as it protected her from the cold winds in the winter.

The Asheville Merchants Association made Jones an honorary member in 1975. She died in 1985 at the age of ninety-two, and her obituary said she was "the last of Asheville's 'flower girls,' mountain women who gathered mountain greenery and wildflowers and sold them to tourists."

After reading the obituary, a woman wrote her thoughts to the *Asheville Citizen-Times*. "It would be wonderful to see this part of the city more full of life and to have more monuments of people and places we would all like to remember," she wrote. "One such monument should be for Emily Jones.... The monument could be located in a flowerbed, like the one in City-County Plaza. I'm sure she would appreciate being remembered by her home town, and it would bring alive some of Asheville's history."

Chapter 11

ROBERT MORGAN'S
HISTORY-MAKING FLIGHTS

If all Robert Morgan had done was fly dozens of World War II bombing runs in the legendary *Memphis Belle*, the Asheville native would have been famous enough. But Morgan found one more way to leave his mark on history.

For years, we thought it was the stuff of urban legend—a widely spread tale that, during a homecoming visit to Asheville in 1943, Morgan flew the bomber perilously low between Asheville City Hall and the Buncombe County Courthouse, in the heart of downtown. Morgan himself had been coy about it, saying in 1979 that despite "speculation" about the incident, he would "continue to refuse to answer" questions about it.

However, in his 1991 memoir, *The Man Who Flew the Memphis Belle*, Morgan came clean about the stunt. But first, he recalled how he and his fellow crew members had logged twenty-five successful missions over occupied France and Nazi Germany, cheating danger the whole way.

In June 1943, the crew left Europe for the United States. A general gave them their orders: "This is your most important mission. You're to go home and thank the American public for what they're doing, and ask them to continue to send us planes and guns and ammunition and all those things they're making in our factories. Remind them that what they have done has made possible what you-all have done."

After stops in several cities including Washington, D.C., Pittsburgh, Cleveland and Mobile, they descended on Asheville. Morgan, who said his "vice" was flying shockingly close to the ground, first buzzed the Biltmore

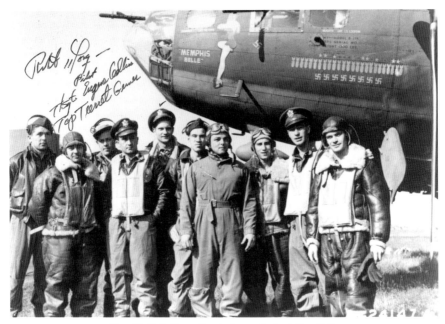

Memphis Belle Crew: Bassingbourn, England: May 1943

(L to R) Harold Loch, Top Turret Gunner; Cecil Scott, Ball Turret Gunner; Robert Hanson, Radio Operator; Jim Verinis, Copilot; Robert Morgan, Pilot; Chuck Leighton, Navigator; John Quinlan, Tail Gunner; Tony Nastal, R Waist Gunner; Vince Evans, Bombardier; Bill Winchell, L Waist Gunner.

Captain Robert K. Morgan of Asheville with the crew of the *Memphis Belle*, Bassingbourn, England, in May 1943. *B027-8.*

Forest Country Club's golf course. "I took the *Belle* down by the 18th hole," he remembered, "low enough that you could have pinged her underbelly with an eight-iron shot, and I noticed that some of the golfers were heading for the woods."

The *Memphis Belle* crew left North Carolina on Saturday, August 14. "Taking off from the Asheville airport…we took off to the north and then turned east up over Patton Avenue," Morgan recounted. "Down ahead of us, on a square at the crest of a gradual rise in the center of town, City Hall and the Courthouse stood, separated from one another by not a whole lot of space at all. 'Oh Boy,' I said to myself. 'Should I go between those buildings?' *Yes*, my self answered. *I think I should*. I figured that a sixty-degree bank would squeeze us through all right. And so, heading east, I banked the plane and put the left wing right down between the Courthouse and City Hall. It was kind of a tight fit, but we made it. Then I turned the *Memphis Belle* left and pulled her up over Sunset Mountain, and we were out of town.

"After dodging flak and Messerschmitts over Germany, flying a B-17 between the County Courthouse and Asheville City Hall was a piece of cake....Rattled a few windows though." (Morgan was far from done: he would go on to fly twenty-six bombing runs over Japan.)

At the time, Asheville City Hall happened to house a U.S. Army Air Force office. "The officer in command of that unit happened to be looking out the window as the *Belle* slanted past," Morgan wrote. "Before we had even reached our cruising altitude he was on the telephone to the Pentagon, sput-sputtering about how Morgan had damn near taken half of greater municipal Asheville with him on leaving the town. As I understand it, the reply he got thoughtfully addressed all his concerns. 'Major Morgan,' the Pentagon officer replied, 'has been given permission to buzz.'"

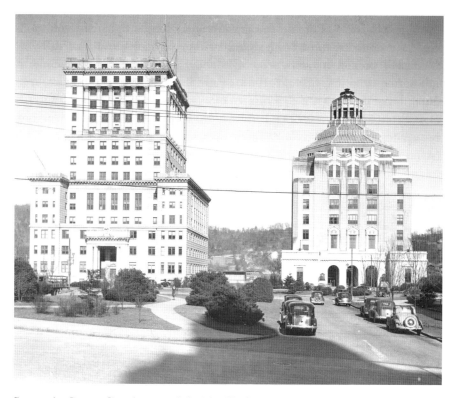

Buncombe County Courthouse on left; Asheville City Hall on right. Morgan uses this photo in his book, and the caption reads: "After dodging flak and Messerschmitts over Germany, flying a B-17 between the County Court House and Asheville City Hall was a piece of cake, even if I did have to bank the plane on a sixty-degree angle. Rattled a few windows though." *H513v8.*

Chapter 12

EVER WONDER HOW ASHEVILLE
GOT TO BE SO COOL? THE 1980S

As you look around downtown, imagine its historic streets and buildings demolished and replaced with a mall. In the 1980s, that's what would have happened if not for the citizens who organized to fight city hall. The story of that decade in Asheville could serve as a primer for citizen activism. Having lived and worked in downtown in the '80s, I feared the story would get lost and forgotten. After discussing it with others who were around during the same period, we decided to put on a program, "Asheville in the 1980s: A Formative Decade Told by Those Who Shaped It." The following account covers some of the highlights of the series about such an important part of our town's history.

When did Asheville's renaissance begin?" We are asked that question a lot in the North Carolina Room, and it's frequently the topic of articles. Most responses turn straight to the 1990s—but native Ashevilleans and those who lived here in the late 1970s and '80s usually see it differently.

It's true that Asheville was in sad shape following its decline from the prosperous '50s, and a lot of effort was required to better it. In 1977, Asheville City Council created a revitalization commission that was charged by Mayor Eugene Ochsenreiter to "get it done." The following year, the council adopted a revitalization plan based on historic preservation and incremental development.

Slowly, things began improving—until March 13, 1980. The *Asheville Citizen* headline that day read, "Giant Downtown Complex Proposed: Plan Includes Hotel, Mall." Through a partnership with a Philadelphia developer,

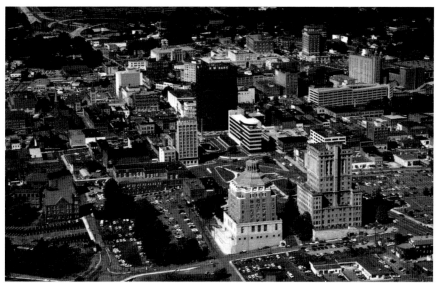

Exciting Downtown Asheville, Land of the Sky   Photo by Jim Doane

Asheville in 1983 after the addition of the Akzona Building (Biltmore Company offices). The reverse reads, "Asheville, N.C. still retains its resort atmosphere while also offering the ability to furnish many big city conveniences." *AA251.*

the plan was to raze eleven blocks of downtown buildings and replace them with a shopping mall.

City council and its revitalization commission had reversed course. Almost everyone, it seemed, was for the mall—including the chamber of commerce, the Housing Authority, the *Asheville Citizen*, WLOS TV, Mission Hospital, the Committee of 36 (a newly formed citizen study group) and the Mid-City Merchants Association.

But not everyone agreed. Opponents organized a group called Save Downtown Asheville, led by downtown business owner Wayne Caldwell. An art installation called *The Wrap*, created by Asheville resident Peggy Gardner, focused attention on the issue by literally wrapping the entire area in cloth to help give people a visual sense of the area to be demolished. Two hundred people volunteered for the effort.

The opponents faced major forces. Vanguard Management Corp. of Atlanta had recently purchased property on Patton Avenue and Wall Street and announced that if the city failed to give solid support to the mall proposal, the firm might withdraw its renovation plans. Council member Walter Boland then announced his solid support of the project, citing the

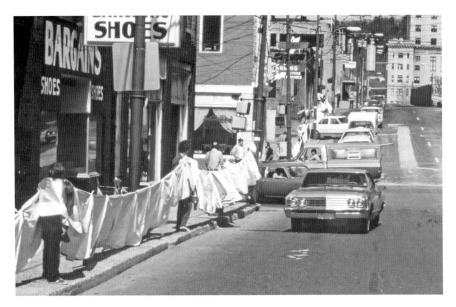

Peggy Gardner's project to "wrap" together in strips of cloth all of the buildings in an eleven-block area that would have been demolished under the Strouse Greenberg & Co. downtown mall complex proposal. Two hundred people participated. Photo by Annie R. Martin, April 19, 1980. *MS218B-04.*

"opportunity to make Asheville a regional retail center, combined with plans for a convention hotel connected to the civic center and for an office complex in the area." He added that it was "an opportunity to do something that would really put Asheville on the map in a very favorable way."

Some seventeen acres, with eighty-five buildings, seemed to be on the chopping block. In November, the Asheville Planning and Zoning Commission voted 5–1 to designate the area as "blighted." The next step was that the city would have to pass a bond referendum to float a $40 million bond. The vote went to the citizens on November 3, 1981, and they rejected the bond proposal for the mall by nearly two to one.

Years later, Caldwell noted that Save Downtown Asheville activists "attended every meeting of City Council, the Housing Authority, Planning and Zoning, and the Asheville Redevelopment Commission. They made notes, spoke at public hearings and civic clubs, asked council for money (which they never got), talked, organized, wrote letters, etc. People gave two years of their lives to defeating a dragon."

A persistent myth holds that, prior to the 1990s, Asheville was "all boarded up." But actually, in 1981, McNally's *Places Rated Almanac* rated the city the number one place to live among 125 small metro areas (under 125,000 population) and number 41 among 277 metro areas of all sizes.

So what was going on here in the 1980s for Asheville to rate so highly? We found five focal points that provide answers: local businesses, social activism, the arts, civic and political engagement and downtown housing and architecture.

BEDROCK BUSINESSES

In 1989, JCPenney became the last department store to leave downtown. But independent local businesses continued to find a foothold. Rob Pulleyn, founder of *Fiberarts Magazine* in 1975 and, later, Lark Books, recalls, "Lower rents and sagging property values in the mid-'70s lured entrepreneurial and pioneering small businesses and made downtown the vibrant and viable place we now see around us."

Some businesses were inherited from the family's previous generation. New entrepreneurs found rents that were dirt cheap. The buildings had nice

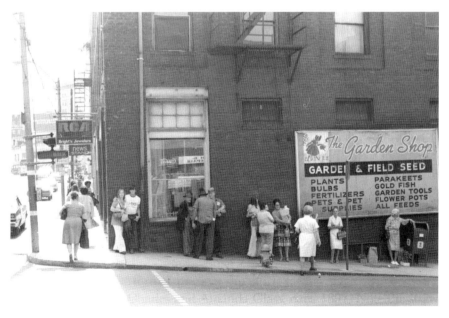

The building at the corner of College and North Lexington. Photo by Rachel Stein, circa 1980. *M445-5.*

architecture, even the boarded-up ones. There was a vestige of a wonderful city under the pall. Though cockroaches were plentiful and the number of customers disconcertingly small, the business owners persisted.

Business people all had their own work to pursue, their distinct challenges to face, but they cared about one another and their roles as downtown pioneers. These courageous souls were the early investors. They invested their time and creative energy and took real financial risks. These people made Asheville viable.

Some examples include women-owned businesses such as Constance's Boutique and 23 Page Restaurant. Though the time period did not make it easy for them, many gay entrepreneurs took a leap of faith and created businesses that drew residents and tourists alike. O. Henry's Bar, established in 1976 on Haywood Street, is the oldest gay bar in North Carolina, and it was likely the first place in town where you could get a sandwich and glass of wine for lunch. Cahoot's Restaurant, Stuff Antiques, Beauregard's Antiques, Futon Design, New Morning Gallery, Malaprop's Bookstore and Café and Jewelry Design were some of the most prominent, and all but two are still in business.

It is also important to remember the cultural diversity that existed downtown at this time. There were the long-standing Jewish proprietors. Greeks also held several generations of restaurants. Pete and Paula Apostolopoulos opened the Mediterranean in 1973. The Shandlers opened the Pickle Barrel in 1978 with a fine assortment of beers and fancy food. Mascari's Stop and Shop was the only place you could buy hummus at the time. The Zourzoukis family's Three Brothers was unrivaled in popularity, as the Pappas family's Five Points Restaurant still is.

Chinese families were here with the long-standing Paradise Restaurant that Thick Fon Lee's family opened in 1947 and operated through 1999. At 20 South Pack Square, long before Pack's Tavern or Bill Stanley's Barbecue, there was Fat Hung Tse's Great Wall Chinese Restaurant.

Hashim Badr, of Jordan, first worked for Eckerd's Drugs downtown, but when it closed in 1982, he realized there was no pharmacy to serve downtown's residents and elderly, so he and his wife, Khawlah "Kathy," opened their own pharmacy, the Asheville Discount Pharmacy. Other members of the family operated the Superette, later renamed the Jerusalem Café. The native Bulgarian Jay Shastri family operated the Windmill European Grill, and Ike Korkman, of Turkish descent, ran the popular Ikes International.

SOCIAL ACTIVISM AND SOCIAL AGENCIES

For more than thirty years, I've heard complaints that there are too many nonprofits in Asheville and they need to consolidate or go away. Asheville has an intricate web of social activism that has been evolving at least since the 1920s. Organizations have come and gone, morphed into new ventures and spun off in different directions. All along the way, there have been businesses, local government and, most importantly, individuals devoted to making life better for people who struggle.

Ellen Clarke and Ann Von Brock, social activists with careers in social agencies, see the history of the 1980s as vital to Asheville today. "Look at the homegrown efforts that took off and how they are influencing who Asheville is today," says Clarke. "The Rape Crisis Center, Children First, Help Mate, Pisgah Legal Services, the Mediation Center, Mountain Housing Opportunities, WNCAP, the anti-nuclear group SANE, the Children's Grammar School, Green Line and the Green Party in WNC, Newfound High School, Peace Link, Manna Food Bank and Western Carolinians for Criminal Justice, to name a few. Many people involved in the early years remember having offices in small spaces offered to them in various downtown

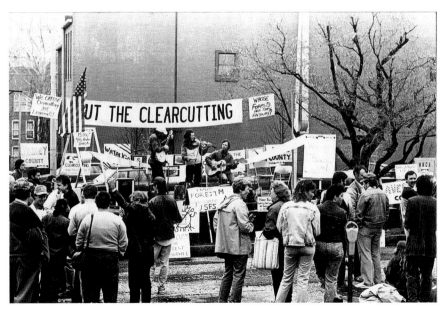

"Cut the Clearcutting" rally, April 15, 1989. Signs read: "We oppose clearcutting not logging"; "Whose Forests Are They Anyway?" The sign above the petition roll reads, "15,000 Say Reduce Clearcutting." *O155-DS.*

churches. We were not resource-rich like we are today—we wore many hats because we were a small community, and there was a lot of resistance, and we banded together."

Von Brock says, "Most other communities in the state were not there yet, in terms of accepting those cutting-edge issues. Asheville wasn't just following what was happening; we were in the forefront."

Asheville in the 1980s was a ripe place for social action. There was a beautiful creativity and boldness that occurred in tackling a problem and figuring out how to partner. It often began as outrage, then concern, finding partners, learning more about the issue and choosing a course of action. This web of social activism still grows and evolves as we continue to face challenges. It is in the very fiber of Asheville.

The Arts: Performing, Visual and Literary

Deborah Austin, head of the Arts Council in the '80s, believes the same thing was happening culturally: "The partnerships that were unique in the '80s were connected with the arts and outdoor celebrations."

In 1982–83, Asheville was in the forefront of the United Arts Fund drive. There were only six other drives in the state, and Asheville raised $100,000.

In July 1986, WCQS broadcast live from Bele Chere. With the stage at the S&W building on Patton, the crowds filled the streets as far as the eye could see. Imagine what these early innovators for downtown must have felt.

"We moved to Asheville in summer 1979 from Illinois, and I thought we were moving to a cultural desert," says Phyllis Lang, former editor of *The Arts Journal*. "Was I wrong! That summer we went to crafts fairs, Shindig and listened to the bands under the trees, several summer theater productions. I was amazed by the cloggers….I went to Pack Library and discovered books by John Ehle and Wilma Dykeman. In September, I started working for *The Arts Journal*, managing the calendar, and once again was amazed at the depth and variety of arts events in the region. Many artists and writers and performers wandered in through the door of *The Arts Journal* on Charlotte Street, and their creativity and enthusiasm convinced me that we had moved to a cultural hothouse."

Connie Bostic, who brought works by Robert Mapplethorpe and Keith Haring to Asheville in her World Gallery and later operated Zone One Art Gallery, commented on the positive role of art criticism at the *Asheville Citizen-*

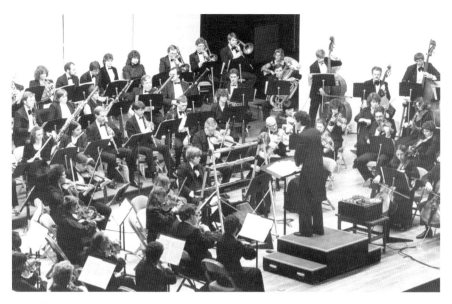

Asheville Symphony Orchestra, with Robert Hart Baker conducting. *1833-8.*

Times. Dancer Ann Dunn agreed that there was a healthy dose of dance criticism in the '80s that pushed the art toward refinement. Dunn's work with the Community Arts Council—a huge outreach program—brought dancers to factories and tobacco barns and to downtown on fire trucks. Dunn worked with schools to bring dance to children. She also recalled that local businesses became involved, assisting with promotional tools and in some cases materials for production.

Ann Whisenhunt, who worked in Asheville's Parks and Recreations Department in the '80s and '90s, said that for her, the richness of the '80s was indeed the "wonderful collaborative spirit that was evident among everybody, among all of the arts organizations, and particularly the City of Asheville's Parks and Recreation Department that had a very strong focus on the arts, and making sure that it reached all of the neighborhoods."

POLITICS AND CIVIL ENGAGEMENT

Leslie Anderson of City Parks and Recreation was hired by the newly formed Downtown Development Office in 1986 as the first Downtown Development director. She can easily see that what was happening in Asheville's arts and cultural community and in social agencies was the same thing that was happening in general with civic engagement. "*Activism*! It's *engagement*, which I think is the hallmark of our community, of what has been our success."

"You had the city, the chamber and you had the Arts Council and you had Quality Forward," Anderson recalls. "We all worked together, and we each had our own piece of it, and we worked for years like that, and it was unique.…When we were trying to get people downtown, we'd try anything. We might have only had ten people show up. But it was the planting of the seeds that over time worked. We knew we had to get people sitting in windows, dining, so when people would drive by, they'd see that."

Soon, the laws followed suit. In 1984, a revision of a city ordinance allowed sales on sidewalks. In 1989, another revision helped encourage outdoor dining and street entertainment.

DOWNTOWN HOUSING

Historian Kevan Frazier believed that you cannot have a strong downtown if you don't have people living in it. He saw the important transformation of creating downtown housing during the '80s as central to its success. In April 1979, the National Historic District for downtown was approved by the U.S. Department of the Interior, another factor in the transformation.

As Frazier recalled:

> *In the mid-1980s, Pat and Roger McGuire renovated 60 Haywood Street, turning the lower floor into shops and the upper floors into apartments with a plan to eventually convert them to condos. The same was done a few years later in several locations by Julian Price and Public Interest Projects, his development company. The work by the McGuires and Price, as well as others, such as David Brown and John Lantzius, demonstrated a new interest in bringing housing to downtown Asheville, particularly through the conversion of abandoned office and warehouse space in the Central Business District. The expansion of housing in this district would come to be one of the key elements of Asheville's renaissance. The tax credits these pioneers utilized saved many of downtown Asheville's architectural gems.*

David Mallet was a pioneer of the downtown Asheville revitalization, opening the Weinhaus, now Asheville's oldest beer and wine store, on Patton

Avenue in 1977. Mallet, visionary that he was, spoke more than thirty years ago to the Pen and Plate Club of Asheville, surmising that "by far the greatest power the city has is its control over building and renovations of older buildings. And it is this area wherein lies the greatest hope for an active downtown. The real solution for downtown is to either 'out mall' the malls or to get people living downtown....Many of the naysayers will say 'who would live downtown?' This is what the city needs and the city has the power to help make it happen. An active, 'alive' downtown, not only from 9:00 a.m. to 5:00 p.m. but from early in the morning to very late at night, is what we are talking about. Not only Monday through Friday, but seven days a week. Can you picture what would begin happening?"

The incorporation of the Preservation Society of Asheville and Buncombe County in 1976 and the creation of the Historic Resources Commission by city council in 1979 helped turn on the lights to the appreciation and preservation of what was already here.

A New Self-Image

During the early 1980s, few of Asheville's residents thought their city had as much to offer as, say, Charleston or Nashville, and fewer dreamed that Asheville would ever rank among the South's top destination cities. But just look what happened!

Asheville's transformation was not the top-down project of a few corporations and a handful of deep-pocket investors. Instead, the city's transformation—and its new awareness of itself—was energized by the grassroots work of literally hundreds of small business owners, local politicians, artists and musicians, social activists and social workers, ad hoc citizens' committees…and countless others.

The cool, creative self-image that visitors sense immediately in today's Asheville didn't just happen. It's a renaissance spirit that dates back to the 1980s.

PART III

CONTRAPTIONS
FROM THE PAST

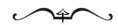

Chapter 13

A WEATHER KIOSK ON PACK SQUARE?

Not long ago, a traveler from Switzerland came into the North Carolina Room to talk about Asheville's weather kiosk. Weather kiosk? Sure enough, the gentleman pulled out several photos of Pack Square that he'd printed from the library's website, and there it was. As familiar as those photos were, we had never noticed the blocky white structure in the center of the square—a United States Weather Bureau kiosk hidden in plain sight.

The Weather Bureau began building kiosks in 1909, equipping them with meteorological instruments and placing them around the country. The kiosks were identical, standing four feet square and nine feet in height. Made of solid cast iron and plate glass, they were set on a granite base. The instruments included a thermometer to record dry temperature as well as a hygrometer to show the degree of humidity. A mechanical barograph drew a line registering barometric variations as they occurred. A rain gauge measured total precipitation while recording the time when the rain fell. The daily official weather map was also displayed.

Asheville wasted no time in setting up its kiosk. The *Asheville Citizen* reported on July 3, 1909, that "the kiosk will be ready for us in the next few days." It assured readers that it "much improves the square and is centrally located making it available to everyone in the city." Civic pride in the kiosk was short-lived, however. City boosters were dismayed to discover that its thermometer registered uncomfortably high temperatures in summer.

A report published by the Asheville Board of Trade in 1914 stated that the average maximum temperature in both July and August was eighty-

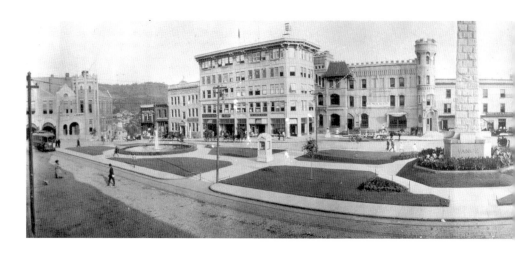

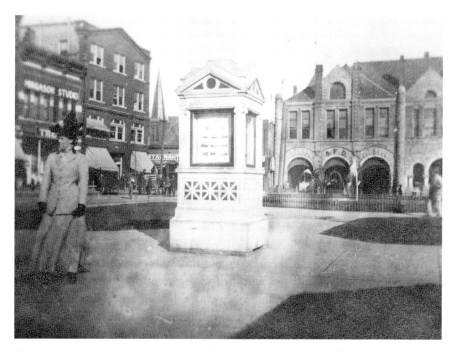

This view of Pack Square, taken around 1910, includes the Asheville Fire Department, city hall, the Vance Monument and the weather kiosk. *L744-4.*

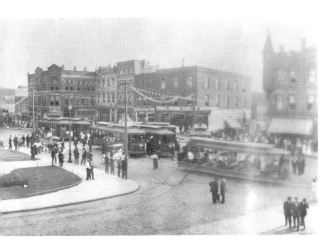

This view of Pack Square, seen from the north, centers on the Vance Monument, with the weather kiosk to its left. The castellated building behind it and to the left was the Pack Library building, 1889–1926. *Photograph by H.W. Pelton, 1910. B440-8.*

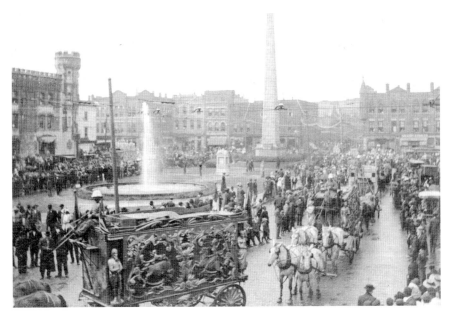

Pack Square during an October 1909 Barnum and Bailey circus parade. The weather kiosk is in full view between the fountain and the Vance Memorial. *B109-4.*

one degrees. Therefore, visitors to the city could escape the "oppressive, enervating conditions accompanying warm weather at lower altitudes." When the readings provided by the new kiosk failed to support this claim, the board began a campaign to discredit it.

"Weather Kiosk Is an Automatic Liar" read a headline in the *Citizen* on August 30, 1909. The high temperatures were blamed on its placement on Pack Square's paved surface, where it had no benefit of shade. "High Temperatures from Radiation Deceptive" the newspaper reported on June 6, 1911, adding that "visitors noting temperature readings would be led to believe the city is hot." Critics further faulted the kiosk for its "beautifully colored pictures of clouds and various explanations, all of which are calculated to catch the eye of the stranger," who would then note the discrepancy. The local weather bureau agreed to put up a disclaimer on the kiosk that read, "On account of local radiation from the pavement and surrounding buildings and from other causes the maximum temperatures recorded here are frequently considerably higher than those of the free air from which official readings are made."

On August 2, 1912, the aldermen discussed whether to move the kiosk to a new location. News coverage of the controversy becomes scarce after this, however, and apparently the kiosk remained in its Pack Square location until December 1919. At that time, the *Citizen* reported that a contract had been issued for the construction of restrooms underground at Pack Square. To clear the construction area, arrangements were to be made "for the removal of the kiosk from the site on which the station will be built. The kiosk probably will be put in some other portion of the square."

No further mention of the weather kiosk appears in the *Citizen*. One can only imagine what became of it after that. Did it move on to a more hospitable city? Was it returned to the Weather Bureau? Was it disassembled by its detractors? We can thank the Swiss traveler for leaving us with this puzzle.

Chapter 14

THIS IS A CARD CATALOG

A college student was interning with the North Carolina Room, and on her first day, we were showing her around, describing the various aspects of the collection. We mentioned that, for historical purposes, we'd kept our card catalog. We noticed she was looking around the room, as if lost. She didn't know what to look for because she didn't know what she was looking for.

With this kind of "card" catalog, you could look up a book by title, author or subject. And if you weren't so great at spelling, you could fudge it—unlike with an online catalog—by flipping through cards for possible alternative spellings.

In March 1994, the Buncombe County Library system turned to an automated online catalog. The project had started in 1988 with a system-wide inventory of books and materials. The State Library of North Carolina granted the Asheville library $100,000 for the project in 1992. Staff attached barcodes to over 270,000 books and re-registered the library's seventy thousand patrons.

The library hired a consultant who finished his report on the conservation and preservation of Special Collections in 1990. Upon this recommendation, an archival database system was purchased, and a part-time clerical staff position was created to assist with data entry. Digitization of the North Carolina Special Collections began.

The information on each of the index cards, such as the one shown here, was typed into a record with a computer-generated ID number. Mind you,

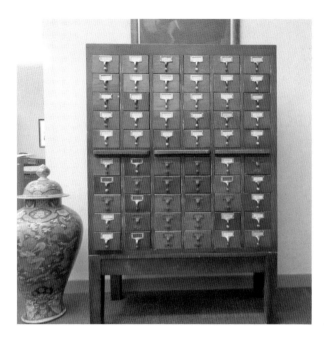

Decommissioned in 1994, the cabinet containing the old North Carolina Room card catalog remains in the room today, evoking bewilderment from young visitors and reminiscences from the older patrons. *Courtesy North Carolina Room.*

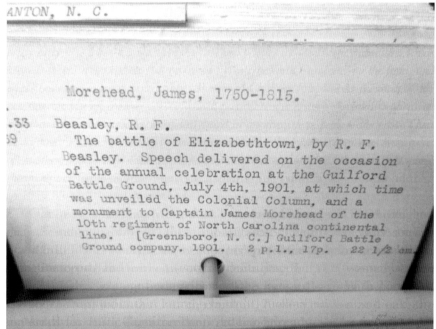

A sample card from the card catalog. *Courtesy North Carolina Room.*

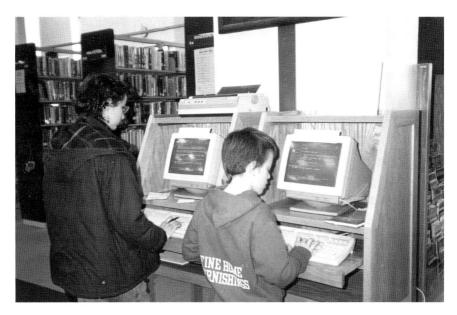

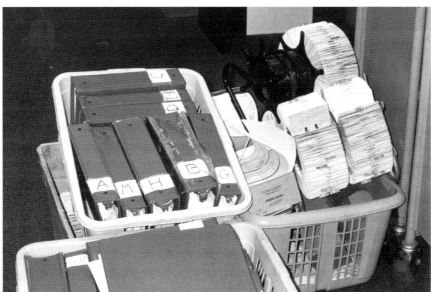

Top: Prior to the catalog's "going live," the public had an opportunity to experiment with the new system. Photo taken in March 1994 by library staff. *MS354.001N image 001.*

Bottom: March 28, 1994: The Dinosaurs—the overdue rolodexes and patron notebooks—are packed up and moved out. *MS354_001N image 002.*

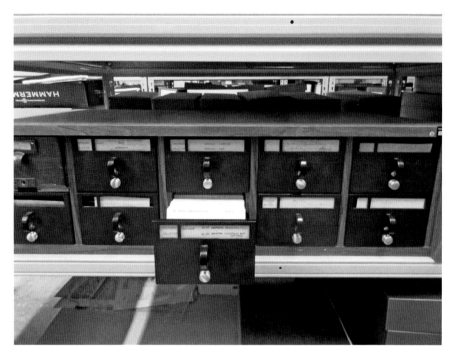

This was the index to our photograph, postcard and special collections. *Courtesy North Carolina Room.*

the information was digitized, but we did not start any scanning of images until around 2001. Prior to scanning in-house, if a patron wanted a copy of one of our images, we sent it to local photographer Tim Barnwell. The patron would then pay for the negative to be made, and their copy and the negative would be returned to us. We first started scanning images for patron requests and then gradually started scanning our collection.

Fifteen years later, in 2016, we have over thirteen thousand photographs and over four thousand postcards scanned and available on the North Carolina Room's website. We've also been working at scanning various manuscript collections, especially photograph albums. Scanning at high resolution is an amazing preservation tool, and making our images available is part of the North Carolina Room's mission. But the next time you expect to find something scanned online, you must know, scanning is not an easy or quick process. My, how time flies.

Chapter 15

FERRY ME TO THE RACES

Items sometimes come to us in the most predestined of ways. A local dealer in rare and quality secondhand books, Chan Gordon, was at an out-of-town book show, and someone he knew showed him a photograph album he had of Asheville in 1908. Chan had no intention of buying it, but as he stood there flipping through the pages, he happened to notice a 4x5 photo of his house at 35 Cullowee Street that fronts on Cumberland Avenue. Built in 1896, the photo of the house was made before two additions were added. Mr. Gordon is probably the only person alive who would have recognized it. He bought the album and donated it to us. The album is one of those rare items of many never-seen-before photographs, including this treasure of a ferry taking horses across the river.

Before there were bridges across the French Broad River, there were ferries. And when bridges were finally built, according to F.S. Sondley's *A History of Buncombe County, North Carolina,* "the Yankee invasion up the French Broad River burned the bridges at Alexanders and at what is now Craggy. For years thereafter between Asheville and Warm Springs ferries were the only means of crossing French Broad River."

So how would someone who lived in Montford in 1908 get their horses across the river to the Riverside Park Horse Show?

Pictured on the following page is a flatboat ferry, and Sondley goes on to say that to "set over" the ferry was "sometimes propelled across by a pole but usually pulled over the stream by a rope stretched at some feet above the surface of the water from an object on one bank to an object on the other bank and securely fastened at both ends. Sometimes the flat-boat

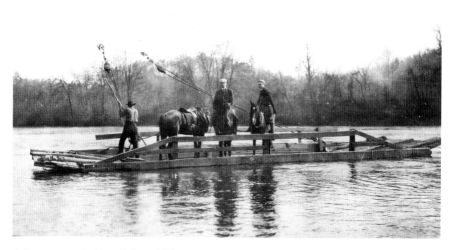

A ferry across the French Broad River carrying two horses and riders. Images are from the Peggy Walker Photograph Album, 1908. *MS283.001A image 3.*

was connected to the overhead rope by another rope fastened at one end to the boat and at the upper end to a large ring through which the upper rope loosely ran; then by turning the front of the boat so that the current of the stream would strike angularly against the boat's upper side the boat would be impelled slowly by the force of the current from one bank to the other bank."

The Sixth Annual Horse Show was held at Riverside Park on April 28 and 29, 1908. The pagoda-style roof on the building to the far left in the image on the top of the facing page is a familiar sight in photographs of the park. The event was a big deal in Asheville, with city schools closing at 12:30 p.m. and city employees calling it an "afternoon holiday." A parade of sorts was viewed from Montford Avenue homes as the procession of horses and traps proceeded to Riverside.

Would there have been other ways to cross the river? Pearson's Bridge was constructed around 1893, located roughly where today's Pearson's Bridge is off Riverside Drive, the first one having been lost in the flood of 1916. The bottom image on the facing page shows the 1893 bridge and the Riverside Park buildings and lakes. The park's location was the stretch of flat land past the bridge at Pearson Bridge Road where Asheville Adventure Center and Smoky Mountain Pallets are today.

We wondered why they wouldn't have used this bridge to take their horses over, but after studying the structure, we thought maybe it was too

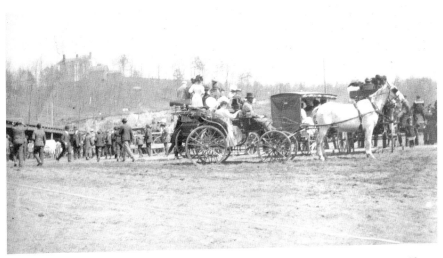

The Sixth Annual Horse Show being held at Riverside Park, April 1908. *MS283 page 10 image 2.*

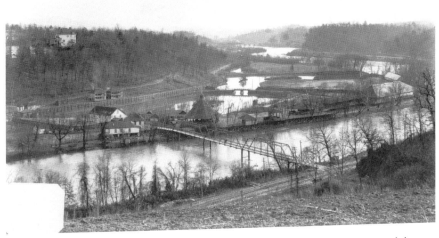

Riverside Park with the 1893 Pearson Bridge across French Broad River. Photograph by John D. Caldwell from original glass plate negative, 1905–10. *B602-8.*

long and narrow for horses. However, looking over additional images in our collection, we were reminded of Pearson's Bridge, which crossed the river right at Riverside Park during the same period. Was the bridge too long and narrow for horses to cross?

Can anyone help us figure out why the ferry—where passengers would have had to pay a toll—was used to cross the horses to the other side, rather than the bridge?

Chapter 16

THE OLD GERMAN CANNON
ON PACK SQUARE

For nearly thirty years, a captured German cannon sat beside the base of the Vance Monument in Pack Square. Then one night in 1942, it mysteriously disappeared. Here is its story.

In the early morning of November 11, 1918, Company I of the 321st U.S. Infantry engaged in one of World War I's final clashes, near Verdun in France. Veterans of the battle included Asheville residents Theodore Sumner and Leftwich Ramsey, who gave thrilling accounts of that day. Three German machine gun nests targeted them, and they threw themselves to the ground to avoid the bullets and cannon fire. Forty-seven men were wounded and fifteen killed. But during the battle, two platoons crept through a swamp until they reached one of the cannons and took possession of it. This helped the soldiers hold their ground until, an hour and a half later, all fighting ceased. The war was over.

The commanding officer, Colonel Dan Adams of Old Fort, ordered the men to lift the three-thousand-pound cannon out of the swamp and onto a wagon. Mules pulled it across France until it was eventually dismantled and crated to be shipped home with the soldiers. Army policy dictated that such equipment should remain in France. However, the cases went uninspected, and so the cannon arrived safely at Fort Jackson, South Carolina. The soldiers who brought it home were then mustered out of the army, leaving it behind. They didn't forget that cannon though. When Colonel Frank Halsted visited Asheville, former soldiers Sumner, Ramsey and Adams recruited him to accompany them to South Carolina to retrieve it. According to reports,

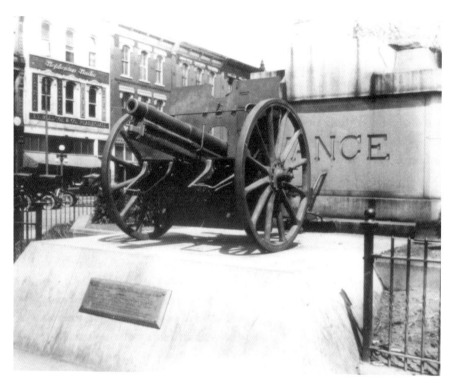

The World War I "Old German Cannon" on Pack Square at the foot of the Vance Monument prior to 1942, the year that it disappeared. *Photo by Ewart Ball. N786-5.*

Halsted used the full authority of his rank to humble the young lieutenant serving as officer of the day at Fort Jackson. Subsequently, the cannon was transferred from a warehouse to a truck and then to the railroad car that brought it over the mountains to Asheville.

The men gave the captured cannon to the city to serve as a monument to the heroes of the Great War. But how would Asheville manage this unexpected gift? Clippings in the Pack Library Newspaper File Collection indicate that there was no consensus. An *Asheville Citizen* article from August 19, 1920, reported that plans were being made for a concrete base to support the cannon but went on to say that "details of the mounting have not been fully determined" and "the exact location is yet to be decided upon." A February 24, 1922 article referred to discussion of the cannon "precipitating volleys and salvos of debate." "A permanent foundation is to be built somewhere, somehow, sometime," but meanwhile, "the old gun has been standing in the rear of the courthouse yard, having been forcibly ejected from the shelter of the county garage several weeks ago."

One year later, veterans' groups took this "point of controversy" to city officials and received approval to place the cannon on Pack Square. They had collected $1,000 to pay for its mounting. On April 23, 1923, a plan submitted by architect Arnold H. Vanderhoof was accepted. His design put the cannon at the base of the Vance Monument on a mount "constructed from gray stone of similar texture." The installation was completed, but apparently some rancor persisted. A January 19, 1924 article reported that the final piece, a bronze tablet commemorating the soldiers' bravery, was placed beside the cannon. However, there was no ceremony to mark the event "owing to the length of time that it has taken to erect the monument and also owing to the fact that a small sum to meet the expense of the mounting had to be raised." It seems that a payment of $73 was still due.

The cannon sat on Pack Square facing down Patton Avenue for nearly three decades. After the controversy concerning its placement subsided, newspaper stories retold its history periodically, celebrating the heroism of the soldiers who brought it home. The cannon was a familiar sight to Asheville residents. But then it disappeared—twice.

The first time the cannon disappeared was in August 1942. An August 26 newspaper article reported that during the previous week, the cannon had been donated to the Buncombe County salvage committee. It was then taken to the army service command depot at Biltmore for shipment to a steel furnace. Adams, now a colonel, protested loudly, sparking "widespread debate," which resulted in the return of the cannon to its base on Pack Square. The reprieve was short-lived, however.

The cannon's second disappearance was reported on October 29, 1942. In the dark of night, it was removed from Pack Square, never to be seen again. Who took it and where it went remain mysteries. However, a note left in its place revealed its probable fate:

> *Dear Folks of Buncombe County:*
> *You won't find me in my accustomed place in Pack Square today. The time has come for me to bid you farewell. My life's story of heroic adventure is now a glorious tradition in this community. You all know me well. I am the old German cannon of World War I that occupied this spot of honor in your beautiful city for 23 years.*
>
> *Although made in Germany I became a loyal American citizen. This is a wonderful country—the home of the brave and the free—and I love it more than anything else in the world.*

That is why I am leaving you—never to return. There is another World War on, fellow citizens, and this time I am on your side. I am made of iron and steel and Uncle Sam needs me.

I have gone to join your boys who are fighting to preserve your freedom and way of life. They need me and I cannot fail them in this critical hour.

If we all do our duty we can save not only America but civilization itself.

Goodbye and God bless you all.

THAT OLD EX-GERMAN CANNON

Chapter 17

Do You Know What a
Fire Alarm Box Was?

B efore it was common for people to have telephones in their homes, if your house caught on fire, you would run to the nearest fire alarm box and pull the handle. Using electric impulses, the box would send a number of tolls on a bell to the fire station, where a fireman would translate the number—in this case #39—and know where the fire was. This box would send in three tolls, then a short pause and then nine tolls, a long pause and repeat itself four times. Register tapes also printed out the number for visual verification.

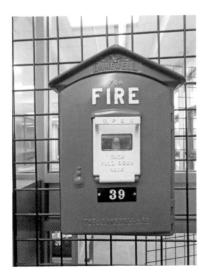

This vintage Gamewell fire alarm box that had been used in Asheville was on display in the North Carolina Room in 2015. *Photo by North Carolina Room staff. O349-DS.*

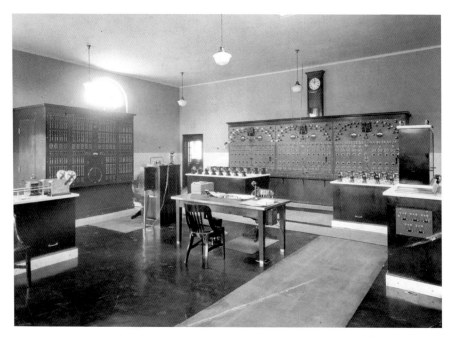

An interior view of the fire department's alarm equipment room; no date given. *A338-8.*

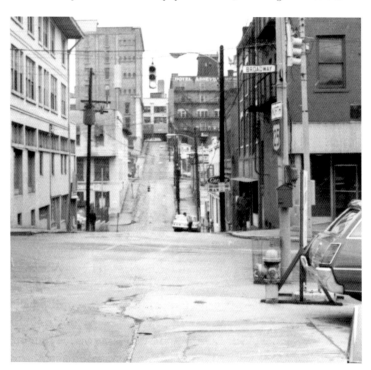

Looking west down Walnut Street from the intersection with Broadway. *Photograph taken by Andrea Clark, 1968. Detail from ACC50-20-DS.*

The fire box system was installed here in the early 1890s and upgraded in 1924, and some monitoring equipment was added in the 1960s. It wasn't until 1987 that the city removed the 114 public fire alarm boxes in the city, citing their incredibly expensive upkeep.

The 1968 street scene in the image on the facing page shows a fire alarm box on the pole to the right.

On December 9, 1986 Asheville Fire Chief John Rukavina reported his findings to the Asheville City Council and recommended that the city's fire alarm boxes be taken down. Less than 15 minutes later he got the go-ahead to remove them. The Asheville system consisted of 107 miles of wire and if there was a short in one of the circuits, some of which were 20 miles long, it could report a short but could not detect where the short was. Thus, it would entail a foot-by-foot visual search of the system. Pranksters were also fond of pulling the alarms, with one-month study showing 28 of 47 calls were false, figured to cost the city $112 per minute per vehicle dispatched.

PART IV

OUTSIDERS, PHOTOGRAPHERS AND MOUNTAIN CRAFTS

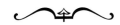

Chapter 18

PHOTOGRAPHERS'
PAINTED BACKDROPS AND PROPS

We've looked at lots of nineteenth-century photographic portraits but have never paid much attention to the backdrops used by most photographers during this era. Apparently, this is a common oversight, as backdrops are a vastly understudied area of photographic history.

Hand-painted backdrops were used for portrait photography from the 1860s to the 1920s. The backdrops, often made with cotton fabric and tempera paint, were a mainstay of the photographer's studio. There were actually awards given at photograph exhibitions for backdrops, props and accessories. The backdrops were often painted by professional and amateur artists or by the photographer. There were also commercial producers of these backdrops; the two largest were L.W. Seavey in New York City and Engelmann & Schneider in Dresden, Germany. Local photographer Ignatius W. Brock, also a famous portrait painter, probably painted his own.

These backdrops, whether commercial or "homemade," were suspended in the studio, and the photographer often had several different backdrops for discerning clients as well as a variety of props (chairs, stools, columns, etc.). Once George Eastman's ubiquitous Brownie became popular, studio backdrops began disappearing because now people could easily have their photograph taken in the real outdoors.

The motif of backdrops ranged quite a bit. Some were of natural outdoor scenery, such as the formal portrait on the following page by James M. McCanless taken of Charles and Amanda Glass, circa 1897. Note the straw on the ground and the elaborate wicker settee. This is likely their marriage photograph.

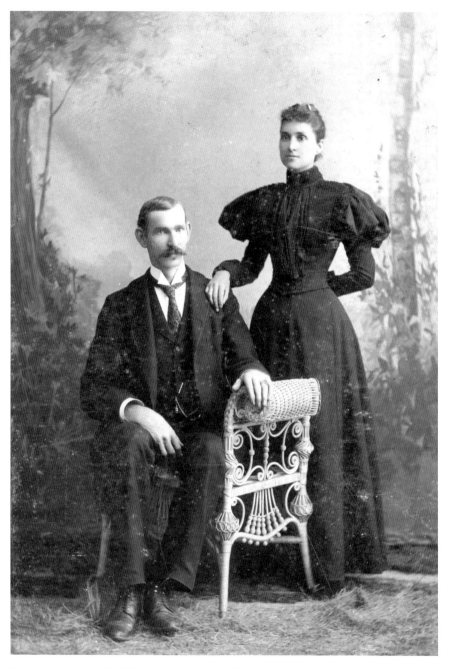

Formal studio portrait of Charles and Amanda Glass seated before a painted backdrop, circa 1900. The photograph was made by photographer J.M. McCanless, whose studio was located on Patton Avenue in Asheville. *K650-5.*

Often, backdrops were quite stately, giving a feeling of opulence, provided most often by the use of architectural elements like arches and solariums. Pedestals and columns, often Greek, were common.

A circa 1896–97 photograph by S.A. McCanless demonstrates this classical-looking background. The only oddity is that the family is posed with a rustic chair and fence. If the family were tourists, wanting to take home with them the rustic flavor of southern Appalachia, we could make more sense of it. But the photo is of Lewis Burgin and Lily Cordelia Deaver McBrayer. McBrayer was an Asheville physician. If the backdrop was meant to denote wealth, was the rustic styling symbolic of something as well? Why the juxtaposition of classical with rustic? Why not use a settee, as in the previous photo?

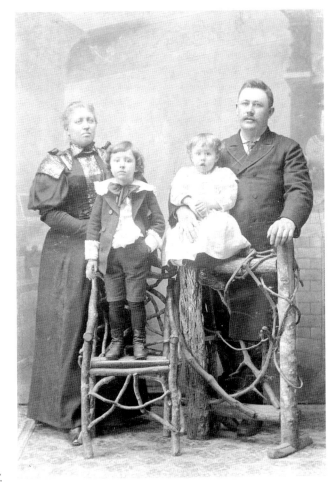

Studio portrait of the L.B. and Cordelia McBrayer family, circa 1896. Photo by S.A. McCanless. *MS242.004EA photo C.*

Here is another use of classical with rustic in a photo by Frank U. Haymond of an unidentified woman circa 1900.

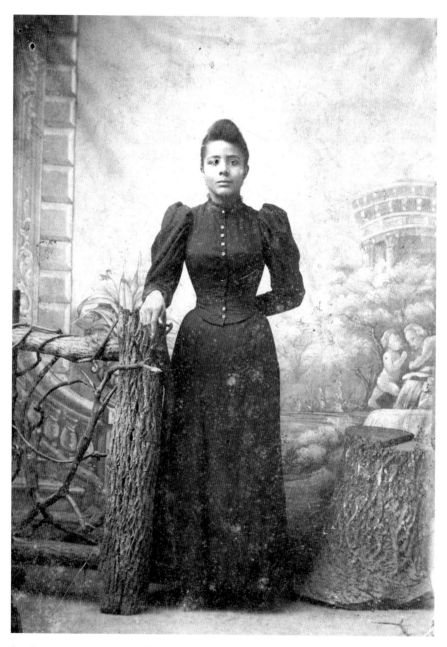

Studio portrait of an unidentified woman posed before a photographer's ornate painted backdrop. The back is stamped "Haymond's Gallery, Asheville, N.C." *L937-5.*

There was also the whimsical use of created backgrounds, such as this photograph by Thomas H. Lindsey of an unidentified little girl posing with a fishing pole, lake and fish included, circa 1900. A mirror on the floor doubles as a small pond. The tree next to her appears to be papier-mâché. A real apple, we think, sits at the toe of her boot.

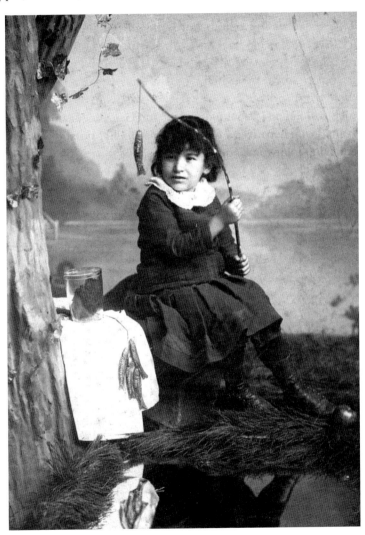

A photograph of a little girl with a fishing pole posed before a painted backdrop. Made at the Lindsey Studio, circa 1900. *K668-8.*

Chapter 19

HIDDEN MOTHER
VICTORIAN PORTRAITS

Sometimes a casual conversation can open your eyes to a whole new world. A North Carolina Room volunteer asked if we'd ever heard of "hidden mother" photographs. We had not, but it piqued our curiosity to find out more.

During the Victorian era, cameras' exposure time was quite long, making it very hard to get good photographs of babies, who were not always the most cooperative subjects. So photographers would often hide mothers behind curtains or other materials, enabling them to hold their babies from behind, keeping them still and calm.

A few days later, we went through the last box of material that a local man, Gary Logan, had loaned to us to scan. It contained a mix of 1880s-era photographs, small family snapshots from the 1940s, folded newspapers, early letters of correspondence, condolence cards, obituaries, school diplomas and calling cards—a good mix of about eight decades of family keepsakes. Included was the photograph on the opposite page of Myrtle and Annie Logan, taken about 1893 by Asheville photographers Lindsey and Brown.

After you look at the children, notice the drapery hanging straight down on the right side. See how it curls toward the smallest child's side on the left and then comes out to drape over whatever the child sits on. Looking at it closely, you might notice the mother's hand coming out of the drapery and resting near the baby's right shoulder. That beige blotch on the other side of the baby may be the mother's other hand, caught in movement by the

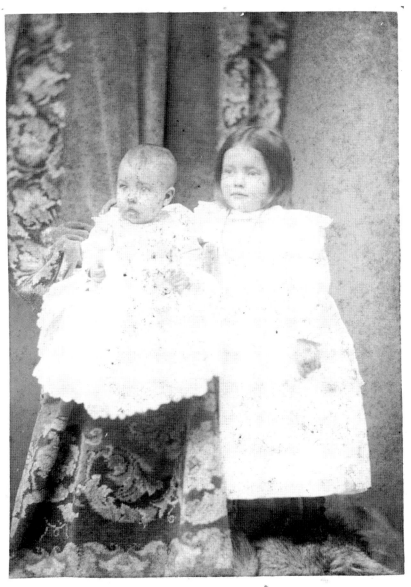

Lindsey & Brown, Imperial Cabinet

SOUTH COURT PLACE.
ASHEVILLE, N. C.

A studio portrait of Myrtle Louisa Logan, *left*, with her older sister Annie, circa 1892. Photographer Lindsey & Brown, South Court Place, Asheville, North Carolina. *MS242.001D photo D.*

camera, or perhaps an attempt by the photographers to blur it out. The mother (who was Rose Addie Deaver, wife of William Erwin Logan) appears to be either standing behind the curtain or perhaps the sheer curtain next to it, or she might actually be sitting with the child on her lap. In either case, the draped material toward the front would cover her legs and feet. A librarian in the Youth Services department believes that the mother's face shows through the sheer curtain. Do you see her?

It was a fortuitous discovery, to be sure—but we so often have such strange experiences in the North Carolina Room that they have become the norm.

In this case, we struck out in search of more hidden mothers, perusing our collection of local baby photographs. This is a photo of Bessie B. Johnson (1880–1972) around the age of two. The daughter of John M. and Harriet Alexander Johnson, Bessie married Daniel "Dan" Earle. The portrait was made by B.A. Culberson. We believe it may also be a hidden mother photograph, with the baby sitting in her mother's lap and her arms draped around, holding the baby.

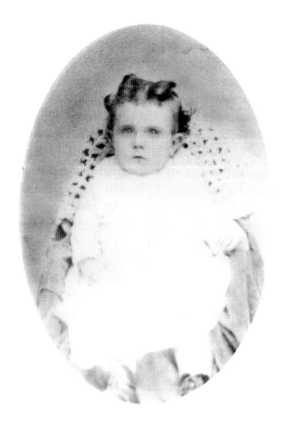

A photo of Bess Johnson, age two, held in her hidden mother's lap. On the back is written: "L.W. Keen Photographer, Jonesboro, Tenn." *MS222.001H photo A.*

In this studio portrait of a young child around the age of two in a white cotton dress, Edna Chandley sits on the arm of a chair draped with material. We believe this is an example of a hidden mother photograph, with the mother behind the material so she is able to hold the baby. Note what appears to be a man's arm and suit sleeve resting near the baby on the left, perhaps the photographer.

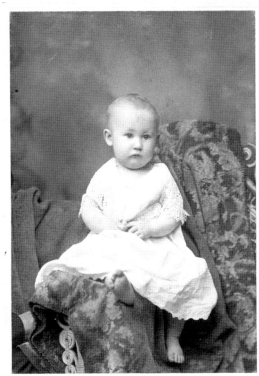

A studio portrait of a young child, Edna Chandley, around the age of two. The draped fabric behind her suggests a hidden mother is holding her. Photo by Lindsey's Art Parlors, Asheville, North Carolina. *MS242.006A.*

Chapter 20

Rustic Furniture Set Against a Modern Gas Stove Demonstration—1905

Several years ago, while researching the Appalachian rustic style of furniture for a lecture and exhibition at the Asheville Art Museum, we came across two intriguing photos in the North Carolina Room. They are from the Caldwell collection of glass-plate negatives given to the library. John D. Caldwell came to Asheville in 1903 to take the position of superintendent of gas operations for the Asheville Electric Company. Among other talents, he was an amateur photographer and documented Asheville history from his arrival until 1944, when he gave many of his photographs to the library. It has been noted that he was responsible for the first demonstration of gas ranges in Asheville.

The images on the facing page appear to portray such an odd juxtaposition. On the one hand, they document a display of new gas ranges. On the other, we see a rustic log cabin interior, filled with furniture and what appear to be small souvenirs on the background shelf and hanging from the ceiling. It's interesting to note that these are wonderful examples of some of the best rustic pieces made in the Appalachians. They are finely crafted, many of them notched for added decoration, and the twig fill is perfect. We only wish that we knew who made them.

Alas, they remain anonymous, but the stage was set for a demonstration of gas ranges (in an electric company showroom—note the electric fan on the stove to the left) by a crisply attired woman standing next to a table covered with bowls and pitchers. Why demonstrate a truly modern object in a rustic space unless the scene was set with this odd juxtaposition in mind— handmade rustic versus machine-made modern?

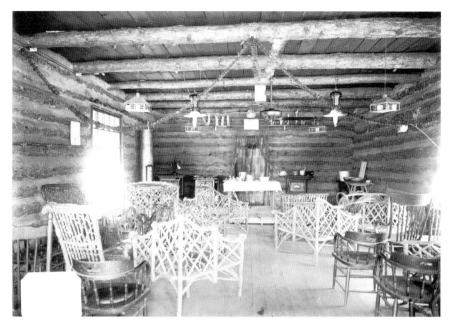

Gas ranges set up for a demonstration inside the Asheville Electric Company's log cabin showroom on Patton Avenue, 1905. *B819-8.*

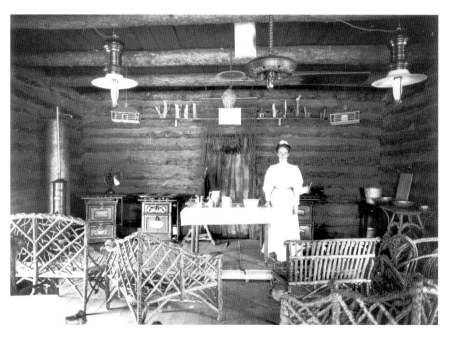

An unidentified woman presents Asheville's first demonstration of a gas range at the Asheville Electric Company's log cabin showroom, 1905. *B820-8.*

Sometimes we just don't have the answers. If this was an impressive debut for gas ranges, you would think that the newspapers would have covered it. But a perusal of the 1905 newspapers brings no mention of this auspicious event. We know that electric stoves were still considered a novelty in the 1920s, while the gas stove had been available since the 1880s, so a gas stove is not surprising in 1905. It also means that Asheville had gas lines available to its citizens. We hear often about the train opening the mountains to settlement and tourism but not so much about the effect of gas and electric lines.

The woman in her light-colored uniform may epitomize the push for cleanliness in food handling, which was a major focus in the early twentieth century. The Pure Food and Drug Act was passed one year later, in 1906.

No matter what the answers, we are left with two fascinating photographs that document a little-known but important demonstration in Asheville history and admire the well-made rustic pieces as well as their counterparts in the machine-made stoves.

Chapter 21

REMEMBERING ARTIST LEROY BAXTER

One of our staff is the proud owner of a Leroy Baxter original. It's a collage made of hearts, diamonds, birds and flowers, reminiscent of the Pennsylvania Dutch, and signed simply "Leroy."

In an exhibit at the North Carolina Room, we featured a mixed media collage by Asheville artist Leroy Neal Baxter. When he passed away in 2011 at the age of eighty-five, his obituary noted, "He had a special artistic skill and would display artwork using a variety of materials."

As Carole Currie tells the story in a July 5, 2000 *Citizen Times* article, "One morning, Baxter was at the right place at the right time, giving away a piece of art to someone at the Mediterranean restaurant when he was spotted by a friend of Charlton Bradsher, owner of American Folk Art and Antiques, 64 Biltmore Ave. The friend sent Baxter to Bradsher and Bradsher bought three of the pieces of art on the spot. Then the amazed and elated Baxter went home to get more pictures." Bradsher called Baxter a "true folk artist" and "the real thing."

Looking for more information about the artist, we found a *Mountain Xpress* article from April 30, 2003, that brought Baxter back to vibrant life. Author Mickey Mahaffey wrote about a morning ride on Asheville city bus #18: "When Leroy Baxter climbs aboard at Oakland and Hibernia, the sleepy passengers become more animated. [Bus driver Jim] Valentine says it's Baxter's job to wake everybody up in the mornings, so they don't

Baxter's collage made of hearts, diamonds, birds and flowers, reminiscent of the Pennsylvania Dutch, and signed simply "Leroy." *Courtesy Nancy Hayes. O345-DS.*

miss their stops. Reminiscing about the old days, Baxter entertains us with lively vignettes of life on 'The Block' back before all the homes were razed. Trolley rides cost 10 cents, and 75 cents bought a big fish sandwich at Breeley's Cafe. Baxter exits at The Mediterranean on College Street. 'If the sun shines again, I'll see you then,' he promises Valentine, hustling into the restaurant before commencing the day's list of odd jobs for assorted downtown residents and business owners."

This collage is a symmetrical design anchored by a large heart, surrounded by flowers and brightly colored shapes, reminiscent of Pennsylvania Dutch symbols. Facing each other are two birds, one bright and cheerful, the other dark and ominous. Glitter and foil paper add sparkle.

In 2008, Baxter showed eighteen of his paintings at the UNCA's Ramsey Library's Blowers Gallery. Publicity for the exhibit stated, "Baxter began making his art a few years ago between jobs as a handyman. Originally he gave away his pieces but began selling them after interest in his work grew around Asheville and the local art scene. Mr. Baxter combines cut-out

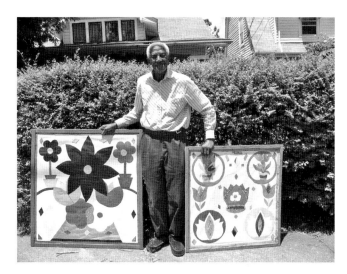

Artist Leroy Baxter
displaying two
of his canvasses.
Courtesy Nancy Hayes.
O344-DS.

shapes, glitter, foil and paint to create pictures that make him happy. He is proud of the pictures depicting churches 'from his mind.'"

Baxter's paintings make us happy too, as does remembering this colorful Asheville character.

Chapter 22

APPALACHIAN RUSTIC SOUVENIRS

I'm a retired curator with a focus on history. I love objects and I love stories. So, it's not surprising that when we moved to Asheville, I quickly became interested in the history of the region. I was also being very cautious about spending money—I'd retired pretty early—so when I came upon my first inexpensive wooden rustic miniature, I was hooked. It was a moonshine still inscribed "Western North Carolina" on the front, and on the bottom, written in pencil, was "Bought at Chimney Rock during the week of my vacation the last of October 1936." Each miniature has a story. As small replicas of everyday things that were once regularly used in an area, they speak to the past. Their inscriptions, whether carved by the maker or added by the buyer, also give us a snapshot of another time in the southern Appalachians. On top of that, they are just plain charming and fun to collect.

The Appalachian Mountains have long been noted for the rugged individualism of their inhabitants. The terrain was and is difficult, limiting its occupants' potential employment. In the late nineteenth and early twentieth centuries, the area was conducive to small farms, cottage industries and the lone artisan. With prevalent rhododendron, mountain laurel, chestnut, hickory, willow and oak, the materials for rustic furniture were at hand, ready to be used in their natural state and suited to an independent craftsperson. For the most part, the work required only rudimentary tools—saws, clippers, pen knives, hammers and measures.

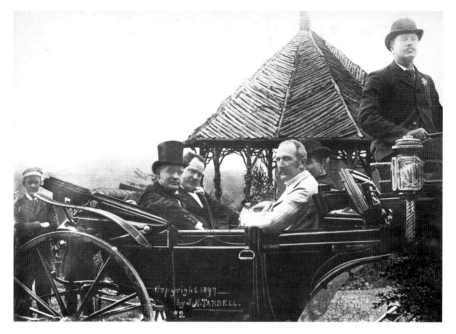

President William McKinley (*in top hat*) in a carriage arriving at the Battery Park Hotel during his visit on June 14, 1897. In view is a rustic structure on the grounds of the hotel. Photo by John H. Tarbell. *A436-8.*

By the late nineteenth century, the trains had arrived in many of the Appalachian areas. With them came tourists seeking the cool air of the mountains and contact with nature. What better way to commemorate their visit than purchasing a locally made souvenir that would remind them of their adventure?

Miniatures are small versions of everyday, normal-sized things. Generally inexpensive and often charming, these pieces made excellent souvenirs, as they were more easily transported from a vacation spot than their full-sized counterparts. Once home, they could be easily displayed or given as gifts. Rustic furniture makers recognized the popularity of these small objects and often inscribed them with their place name. The small rustic chair inscribed "Asheville, NC 1904" was a staple of many rustic furniture builders. These chairs were modeled somewhat on the full-size chair known regionally as a "settin' chair."

As with much of Appalachian rustic, whether miniature or full-sized, the chair is notched to give decoration. Many of these souvenirs were sold over a long period of time. The miniature wishing well and the moonshine still are

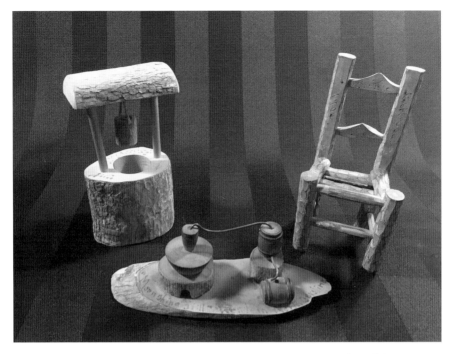

Three miniature pieces of rustic souvenirs. *Courtesy Lynne Poirier-Wilson. O348-DS.*

both from the 1930s. The still, inscribed "Moonshine Still Asheville, NC," also has a notation by the original purchaser penciled on the base—"bought at Chimney Rock during the week of my vacation the last of October 1936." All three of these objects have been found in catalogs of the Treasure Chest, an Asheville company that sold Appalachian crafts.

Chapter 23

HUGH BROWN, THE TREASURE CHEST AND THREE MOUNTAINEERS: SOUTHERN MOUNTAIN CRAFT INDUSTRIES

A beautiful woman with silver-gray hair and bright red lipstick walked into the North Carolina Room one day and began fumbling in her purse. She pulled out a piece of folded paper, handed it to me and said that she would like for us to add this to our files. She told me that her father, Hugh Brown, and his work with handicrafts was involved.

I opened the paper and saw that it was typed minutes, titled "Exposition of Mountain Arts & Crafts," from a meeting held in the auditorium of the chamber of commerce on July 14, 1925. People present were listed: "Bishop Junius M. Horner, President; F. Roger Miller; Miss Jean S. Fuller; Mrs. Mary Martin Sloop; Mrs. M.E. Marsh; Miss Clementine Douglas; Mrs. Helen T. Nichols; H.C. Brown; William W. Dodge, Jr. and Charles J. Harmon."

The object of the meeting, as explained by Mr. Miller, was to have an exposition to present to the tourists and visitors of Asheville an opportunity to learn more about the industries carried on by the people of the North Carolina mountains and to give the public a chance to purchase the handicrafts. He thought it important "for them to see the loom, the spinning wheel, the potter's wheel, etc."

Charles H. Honess, an optometrist, offered his building at 54 Patton Avenue, and the date was set for the exhibition on August 17–31, 1925. Mr. Dodge and Mr. Brown were to attend to making tickets and stationery and other advertising; Mr. Miller said the chamber of commerce had agreed to do the publicity.

People at the meeting subscribed to floor space and agreed to provide demonstrations for the following: "Mrs. Sloop of the Crossnore School a weaver; The Appalachian School [of Penland] a spinner; Miss Douglas a hooked rug maker; Allanstand Cottage Industries a basket maker; Mr. Brown a potter at his wheel; Mr. Dodge a display of hand wrought silver; Mrs. Lynch to show homespun material from the Grove Park Inn," and they would try to have the Tryon Toy Makers wood carvings present. It was suggested "there be some entertainment making a feature of Mountain songs and folk dances."

I had never seen reference to this exposition, and I knew that this networking was earlier than the beginnings of what the Southern Highland Guild's history recounts, which references many of the same people meeting together at Penland in 1928 to form the guild chartered in 1930. Anyone familiar with the Southern Highland Guild Fair will see the similarities to this 1925 expo.

I had to swallow my pride and tell the woman that I was not familiar with her father, Hugh Brown, or his work.

Eleanor Brown Hall, the eldest daughter of Hugh Brown, was the woman who had handed me the minutes. We became close friends over the next decade as she led me through all that she knew, introduced me to her three siblings and took me to interview people who were still living who had known her father. I would learn that she was the torchbearer of her father's work, which I continued to research for several years.

The free two-week exposition was held, with both newspapers covering the event. The first week alone brought "thousands" to the exposition. Cherokee crafts were also presented, and both O.L. Bachelder's Omar Kyayynam and W.B. Stephen's Pisgah pottery were at the exhibits.

Hugh C. Brown was an Asheville native. Born in 1884, Brown was sixteen years old when Asheville author Thomas Wolfe was born. Hugh Brown's Asheville was Thomas Wolfe's Asheville. Brown grew up on College Street, a block one direction from Wolfe's birthplace on Woodfin Street and a block the other direction from Wolfe's mother's boardinghouse on Spruce Street. Hugh Brown did not finish high school but started working at a young age to help support his parents. After working for the Asheville Hardware Company on Pack Square, he opened the Brown Hardware Company at 25 Broadway in 1911.

After building that business into one of the largest hardware concerns in Western North Carolina, he tired of pushing hardware and started a gift shop within his hardware store. By 1924, Hugh Brown had expanded his

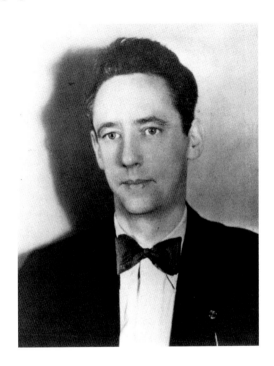

A formal portrait of Hugh C. Brown, owner of Brown Hardware Company (1911–31) and the Treasure Chest (1924–31) and president and co-founder of Three Mountaineers (1932–92). *M981-8.*

gift section, and he opened it then in its own building and christened it the Treasure Chest.

The Treasure Chest was also known as "The Dinnerware House of Asheville," and many Asheville residents remembered that when you got engaged, you went down to Brown's to pick out your china. An *Asheville Citizen-Times* article describing the opening of the Treasure Chest said that visitors passed before "sixty tables of sixty various china patterns that were on display." The newspaper also reported that "local objects are not lacking. A prominent part of the display is the rack of Rhododendron pottery and another, devoted to the coarser ware produced at Jugtown, near Canton." Mountain-made handicrafts were offered to the large number of tourists as "souvenirs from the mountains."

Hugh Brown founded a woodworking business, Blue Ridge Woodcrafters, in 1922 to supply the Treasure Chest with some of the wood novelties and furniture. Cecil V. Clayton was in charge.

One year after the opening, the Treasure Chest began advertising in three national magazines: *House Beautiful, House & Gardens* and *American Home Magazine.* Brown developed the Treasure Chest merchandise for several years, creating a wholesale business as well as the retail store. The first catalog was produced in 1928.

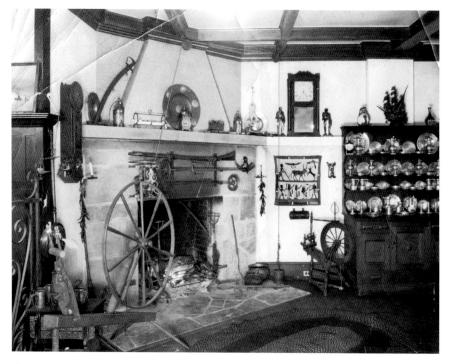

Above: Interior of the Treasure Chest believed to be around its opening on December 1, 1924. *N917-8.*

Opposite: *Treasure Chest* 1928 catalog, page 59. *MS082.001Q*

The Treasure Chest also sold hooked rugs, which it trademarked as "Aunt Nancy Hooked Rugs." Numbered tags with the Aunt Nancy logo were attached, but not directly to the rugs. Within the company's first year, it began wholesaling the rugs to jobbers in New York City and to department stores in large metropolitan centers. The Treasure Chest went from selling ten to fifteen hooked rugs a month to selling about three hundred hooked rugs a week at the beginning of 1926. Between 1926 and 1927, more than fifty thousand hooked rugs were sold, according to local press reports.

Hugh Brown had an eye and appreciation for Colonial Revival wares. He visited the American Wing of the Metropolitan Museum in New York in 1926 but wrote to his wife, Lelia, on March 8 that he did not find a thing that he "could make use of with the exception of a pair of andirons and they looked like a copy of the ones I had already planned to market."

Other businesses, both in Asheville and across the Appalachians, worked to sell mountain-made crafts, and the Treasure Chest was not the

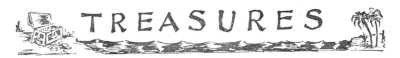

T R E A S U R E S

H A N D - W O V E N   T H I N G S

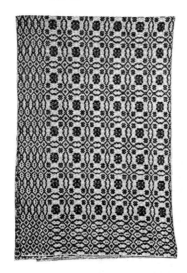 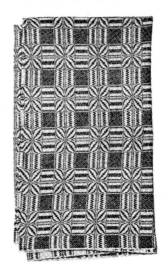

OLD-FASHIONED COVERLETS

The "Whig Rose"

Is one of the oldest patterns in American weavings as it dates back to the American Revolution. This coverlet is hand-woven and is all wool, it is made in both full and twin bed sizes. Colors, Blue, or Old Rose.

No. 865 Full Size.
No. 866 Twin Bed Size.

The "Reed Leaf"

This too is an old pattern and a very pretty one, both it and the "Whig Rose" remind one of the old ones that our grandmothers had. Wool materials in two sizes and colors. Blue, or Old Rose.

No. 870 Full Bed Size.
No. 871 Twin Bed Size.

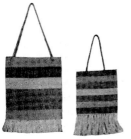

No. 8-R   *No.* 5-R

Hand-Woven Bags

The folks that make these bags call them "Rainbow" bags owing to the lovely rainbow colors used in the many stripes. They are nice for a lady's coin purse, compact, and handkerchief and add a touch of color to the ensemble. Two sizes, small one No. 5-R 5"x5". No. 8-R 8"x8".

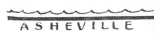

A S H E V I L L E   NORTH CAROLINA

first. Frances Goodrich, who established one such early organization, the Allanstand Cottage Industries, was located first in Madison County and then in a shop in Asheville in 1908. Goodrich, known for breaking ground for establishing a national market for mountain handicrafts, knew that the aim must always be to increase their market, as she wrote in a "Letter to the Stockholders 1/28/1925," found in the Southern Highland Handcraft Guild Archives.

The success of the Treasure Chest lay in its marketing. The Treasure Chest sold its merchandise in the Asheville shop, but it also developed relationships with representatives in the gift trade across the United States. The Treasure Chest attended the spring and fall shows of the National Gift and Art Association, which were held in major U.S. cities such as Boston, Philadelphia and New York.

The Treasure Chest prospered and supplied work for hundreds of mountain families, provided employment for the representatives and also "was responsible in part, for the growth of several local potteries—Jugtown and Stephens." "Stephens" refers to Walter Stephen, who founded Pisgah Forest Pottery, and "Jugtown" refers to the pottery near Candler in Western North Carolina that was operated by William Penland.

On November 20, 1930, the Central Bank and Trust Company of Asheville failed to open its doors. The bank went under and took Hugh Brown with it, as it did many other businesses. Before Hugh Brown's case came to court, he wrote to a close associate and New York representative, providing an interesting historical analysis of what happened to many businesses during this time: "The Treasure Chest on the first day of January this year, after overcoming the fact that all their assets were tied up on November 20th in a closed bank wound up the year without owing a penny to a soul in the world."

Hugh Brown also assured his friend that "if he should lose in court the next day," he wouldn't be looking for a job. "I am going to make one, and I am still as deeply interested in Mountain Handicraft's as ever, and you will see me bob up again before many moons." Hugh Brown did lose both Brown Hardware and the Treasure Chest. The Treasure Chest went into receivership, with the court appointing a receiver to continue to operate the business.

THE THREE MOUNTAINEERS

Hugh Brown had lost all that he had worked twenty-one years to achieve. However, literally on the heels of the Depression, with a wife and four children to support, Brown did as he said he would and joined with his brother Edwin and previous employee William H. Lashley and founded Three Mountaineers. All three men were born in the Blue Ridge Mountains, hence the name. Their total starting capital was $500. To begin, they obtained "four loads of pottery and it was not until some of this was sold at retail for cash that they were able to make the small deposits required to have the lights and water turned on at their new location at 205 College Street." The company again dealt almost exclusively with mountain products such as handmade pottery, hooked rugs and baskets, according to the *Three Mountaineers, 1972 Fortieth Anniversary Catalog.*

The Blue Ridge Woodcrafters, which Hugh Brown had been able to hold on to, continued to supply wooden products. Brown returned with his new line to the National Gift and Art shows. He renewed his business relations with some previous sales representatives and formed relationships with new ones.

Three Mountaineers now had to compete with the Treasure Chest. Confusion often arises from the name of the Treasure Chest between the business that was begun by Hugh Brown and the one that continued to be in existence after he lost it. Many local crafts people who supplied crafts for the Treasure Chest were not aware of the change in ownership. After the court-appointed receiver operated it for about a year, it was operated by Frank M. Weaver Jr. and was still later incorporated in 1940 by the Farmers Federation, becoming the Treasure Chest Mutual, Inc. It stayed in operation until 1956.

The new and struggling business of Three Mountaineers was not able to put out a catalog until 1936, and even then, it had to send it out in two parts.

Just six years after beginning Three Mountaineers, Hugh Brown died in 1938, at the age of fifty-four. It is likely that overwork contributed to his early death. An editorial in the *Asheville Times* on June 23, 1938, read, "When the depression exacted its tribute of him, as it did of so many others, he paid it unwhimperingly and started anew, courageously erecting a new business on the ruins of the old." The total net worth of the business at this time was approximately $16,000.

William H. Lashley took over management. In 1939, Blue Ridge Woodcrafters was merged into Three Mountaineers, and Cecil V. Clayton became a stockholder in the company. Due to wage and hour laws enacted in 1940, the company discontinued handling local native crafts and turned exclusively to manufactured wood products. The business grew rapidly, and sales reached a total of $265,000 in 1941.

William Lashley, who was working for Hugh Brown by 1924, was responsible for almost all of the designs of the early handicrafts as well as the later, machine-made items. He produced all of the company's catalogs, hand drawing the early ones.

Three Mountaineers, even after surviving the loss of its founder and the Depression, suffered its most difficult financial crisis during World War II. Employees were drafted and materials were almost unobtainable. After surviving the war years, the business suffered a devastating fire in 1951 that almost totally destroyed 205 College Street. A new plant was built in 1953 on land purchased earlier on Thompson Street in Biltmore near the Swannanoa River, eventually expanding into a 225,000-square-foot factory. The product line continued to grow, with large pieces such as hostess carts and beveled cheval mirrors to more mainstay products like spice cabinets, snack tables and magazine racks.

William H. Lashley retired from the company in 1964 with a payroll of 225 employees. During the energy crunch of the mid-1970s, the company turned its byproduct into fire logs by compressing sawdust under pressure. Employment peaked at 250 during the end of the 1970s. Throughout the company's history, Three Mountaineers contributed to the local community in many ways, providing employment for hundreds of people and giving college scholarships to employees. Many Ashevilleans retired from the company with twenty and thirty years' employment.

Ever able to overcome difficulties, Three Mountaineers finally succumbed to the combination of foreign competition in the furniture market, changing tastes in home furnishings and a lingering recession. In 1992, Three Mountaineers closed after sixty years of operation.

Chapter 24

THE CABIN KIDS

Who remembers the Cabin Kids? These six Asheville singing talents performed across the country and found Hollywood fame. Other cities claim the family, but we have been able to find further important historical information to back up our claim.

Four of the Cabin Kids' parents were James and Anna Coleman Hall, who moved to Asheville from Newberry, South Carolina, by 1922. Before leaving, their first child, Helen, was born in South Carolina in the same year. Anna then gave birth to James Joseph Hall in Asheville in 1923. Another child born in 1925 died at the age of one. Winifred was born in 1927, and then Frederick Hall was born here in 1928. Anna and a baby died during childbirth in December 1930.

The following year, James Hall married Beatrice Beaty, and she treated the children as her own. Beatrice was the daughter of Henrietta and John W. Beaty, pastor of New Bethel Baptist Church on South French Broad in Asheville. James and Beatrice Hall were living in West Asheville on Mardell Circle in 1932, when Beatrice first started taking her adopted children to perform at area civic clubs and theaters, including a performance on the Grove Arcade rooftop and at the George Vanderbilt Hotel for the Kiwanis Club.

Initially, the group called themselves the Jolly Six Sextette. They included four Hall children—Helen, James, Winifred and Frederick—and two children from Beatrice's neighborhood on nearby Buffalo Street, Edward and Theodore Chavis, sons of Theodore and Anna Chavis. Beatrice was the accompanist and director.

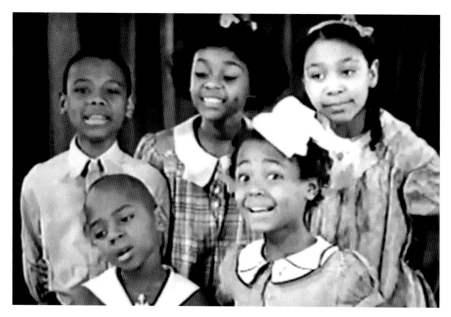

The Cabin Kids. *Public domain; source unknown.*

Besides local performances, by 1934, out-of-town singing tours included stops in Franklin, Waynesville, Canton and Tryon, North Carolina; Spartanburg, Greenville and Columbia, South Carolina; and Knoxville and Bristol, Tennessee, with a two-week engagement at Charleston and Bluefield, West Virginia, according to the *Asheville Citizen* of April 13, 1934.

After a man from New York by the name of Harold Kemp heard them sing in Hendersonville in 1933, he made arrangements the following April for the group to appear on a fifteen-minute radio program over station WRC in Washington, D.C., an affiliate of NBC network. They sang on the radio as the Cabin Kids. An *Asheville Citizen-Times* article in 1934 identified the members, which no longer included the Chavis children but added Ruth Gamble, who was born in 1923 and was the daughter of Frank and Flora Gamble, who lived next door to the Chavis family. The WRC broadcast got the group a "year's contract for appearances in New York City and one of six months in Hollywood," as reported in the *Citizen* on May 27, 1934. They gave their final Asheville appearance the following Friday at the Negro YMCA on College Street. In addition to Ruth Gamble, the group now included Martha Pearson.

And they were off. Following the radio program, they were given motion picture contracts, first appearing with an important bit in *Mississippi* with

Bing Crosby, W.C. Fields and Joan Bennett. The show opened in Asheville at the Imperial Theater in March 1935. The Cabin Kids also appeared on WWNC in September 1935. They became known and loved for their singing and comedy skits. After singing in several Hollywood productions over a couple of years, the kids and James and Beatrice came to Asheville in March 1937, staying at the home of physician Herbert N. White, at 69 Madison Street. They left here for Johnson City, Tennessee, returning to the big time, where their talents were featured in many films, shorts and television shows, including *The Little Rascals*.

James Hall, along with children Helen, James, Winfred and Fredrick, was in New Jersey in 1940. James, widowed, listed his occupation as a manager in theatrical work. This points to the idea that Beatrice had died and James had taken over as the manager. The Cabin Kids performed at many impressive venues, including the Apollo Theatre, and in more than twenty movies and short films with Hollywood's biggest stars, including Bob Hope, Bing Crosby, Roy Rogers, Buster Keaton, Shirley Temple and Danny Kaye.

After the group outgrew the Cabin Kids, the sisters in the mid- to late '40s went on to perform as the Hall Sisters, and a family member reported that Ruth (Sweetie), Helen (Precious) and Winifred (Sugar) performed in Cuba and at the Apollo, as well as touring with the USO during World War II. A ship passenger list shows that Helen and Winifred and Ruth Chavis left Plainfield, New Jersey, for Yokohama, Japan, in June 1946. Ruth Chavis's birthdate of July 9, 1922, on the register is the same as Ruth Gamble's birthdate, so it is assumed that Ruth was married by this time.

The Hall Sisters cut a record with Jesse Stone and His Orchestra on the RCA Victor label with "You Never Can Tell the Depth of a Well (By the Length of the Handle on the Pump)" (Green-Coben-Meisher). The Hall Sisters were the first to release, also with Jesse Stone, "Trouble Is a Man" in 1947.

The Bill Board: The World's Foremost Amusement Weekly, dated September 6, 1947, described their sound: "The trio harmonies of the Hall Sisters, their voices shrill and without body in their blend, brings no provocation to their initial plattering. Nor does the music making of Jesse Stone's band add any more rhythmic flavor or color to their chanting. Their sepia qualities pronounced in their singing and in the band's playing, gals fare better when piping to the bounce beats for an innocuous 'You Never Can Tell' than when singing it slow and close for the 'Trouble' blues dirge."

Chapter 25

SWANNANOA WOOD CARVER
WADE MARTIN CARVES ONE LAST PIECE

Wade "Gob" Hampton Martin was born in 1920, the son of Marcus Lafayette and Callie Holloway Martin. He had four brothers (Edsel, Wayne, Fred and Quintin) and one sister (Zenobia). All of them carved wood.

In the early 1930s, the family moved from Andrews, North Carolina, to Swannanoa. Wade was nine at the time and grew up in Beacon Village. After serving in World War II, Martin got a job at the Beacon Manufacturing Company. In 1950, he took some carvings to Margaret Roberts, the manager of Allanstand Craft Shop in Asheville. When she sold those, Martin carved more. In her article "The Carvings of Wade Martin" in *May We All Remember Well*, Vol. 1, Maggie Lauterer wrote that when Martin got laid off at Beacon, he started carving full time. He found he could make more money selling three carvings a week than working in the mill.

Martin was a master craftsman who sold his pieces all over the country and won national acclaim. The *Asheville Citizen-Times* would note in 2007 that his "original carvings sold for $25 or less and were often given as gifts or bartered in exchange for medical or dental care. Many sell for thousands of dollars today. A set of four small musical figures recently sold at Brunk Auctions in Asheville for close to $4,000."

Martin started carving less and less in the late 1980s and had basically stopped by 1993. And then, Algene "Genie" Larae Ott asked him if he'd make one more carving, a carving of Smokey Bear signing "I love you."

And so he did.

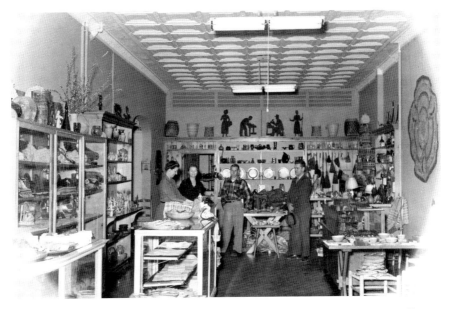

The Allanstand Mountain Craft Shop, including (*left to right*) shop manager Margaret Rose Roberts, Gertrude Bader, Wade Martin and William Carl Bader, April 1952. *K351-8.*

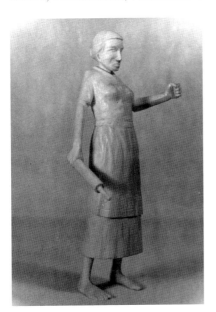

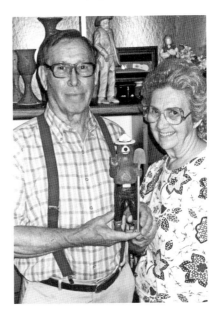

Left: *Woman with Rolling Pin*, a wood carving by Wade Martin for sale at the Allanstand Mountain Craft Shop, 1955. *K346-5.*

Right: Wade Martin holds his wood carving of Smokey Bear while his wife, Frances Martin, looks on, 1993. Photo by Bob Ruiz. *MS256.002A photo A.*

PART V

THE COMING AND GOING OF SACRED PLACES

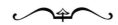

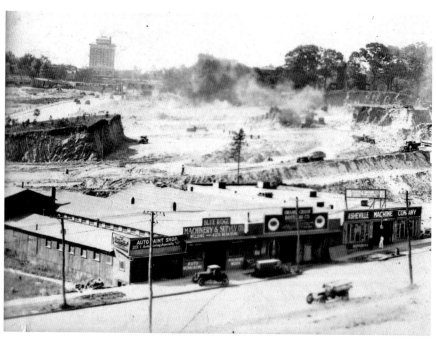

Demolition of Buxton Hill in 1926. The entire hillside above Southside Avenue from Coxe Avenue (*on left*) to the intersection with Church Street (*on right*) was excavated in order to add two new streets and create the Buxton Hill Development. *O095-DS from the Aaron Mundy Collection MS285.*

Chapter 26

SOUTH SLOPE: THE DEMOLITION, 1926

In the spring of 2015, the North Carolina Room received on loan one of its largest—and most enigmatic—photograph collections of early twentieth-century Asheville.

When Weaverville resident Judson "Buster" Mundy passed away in 1981, he left a large passel of old, slightly discolored photographs tucked away in his barn. Thirty years later, his grandson Aaron Mundy found the pictures and sensed they might be of historical interest. The assortment included a "Souvenir Album" of Barnhill Studio photographs of the 1916 flood of the French Broad River, but almost all of the other items were undated, and for the most part, the subjects were unidentified. Aaron guessed that someone might recognize the street scenes, but where to go? At the behest of his friend Dennis Dixson, Aaron contacted the North Carolina Room and asked whether we might want to borrow the photographs to scan and add to our collection and, in the process, help him identify some of the views.

Two of the photographs led us on a merry chase for clues and background, ending in blog posts that generated a lot of reminiscing and local conversation. Those posts are included in this book: "South Slope: The Demolition, 1926" and "Grace: A Community that Got Absorbed by an Avenue."

At first glance, the photograph opposite gives few clues as to precisely where or what this was, other than that it appears to be a massive construction site in Asheville. The automobiles and old construction equipment hint at the 1920s, but what was being demolished, and where?

We searched the Asheville city directories. There, in the 1926 edition, was the listing for the businesses in view: Asheville Machine Company, Orange Crush Bottling Co., Blue Ridge Machinery and Auto Paint Shop—all on

Southside Avenue. The directory listed Asheville Machine Company at 51–53 Southside. With a magnifying glass, we looked closely at the numbers on the building. Sure enough, the numbers 51 and 53 appear by the door of Asheville Machine Company.

So this was Southside Avenue, circa 1926. But what was the demolition? Could this have been the continuing construction of Coxe Avenue?

We ran the digital image through a few Photoshop filters and zoomed in, hunting for another clue. We found it. On the horizon, below the Battery Park Hotel, we spotted a building marked "J. Gorham Low." Bingo! The directory indicates that in 1926, one Mr. Low, who owned an Exide car battery shop on Biltmore Avenue, opened an additional shop on the newly created Coxe Avenue, near the corner of Hilliard Avenue.

This told us that the street in view, in the upper left corner, was Coxe Avenue, and that because it had traffic it had already been completed. So, the demolition was not for Coxe Avenue.

Searching our database for photos of Coxe in the 1920s, we found an aerial view of Asheville shortly after the avenue was built. And there, just east of Coxe and north of Southside, was a hillside of woods and farmland.

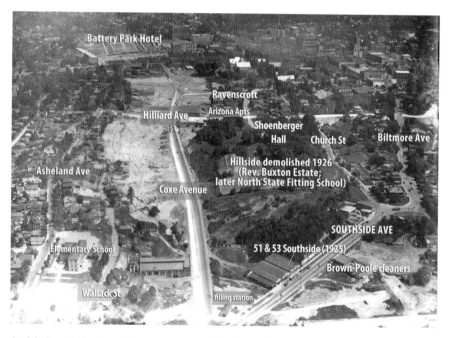

Aerial view of the Coxe Avenue area soon after the road was created, circa 1925–26. Buxton Hill is the farmland and woods just above Southside Avenue. The hill would be leveled about a year after this photo was taken. *A019-8.*

Zooming in on the buildings in the lower right-hand corner, we see that in fact they are the same shops that appear in the prior photo. The buildings match, right down to the large sign on top of the Asheville Machine Company. What we see in the construction photo is the creation of what we now call South Slope: Millard, Buxton and Banks Avenues were all carved out of that hillside.

We asked historian and architectural designer Dale Slusser, "Did the hillside have a name?" The answer: Buxton Hill, of Thomas Wolfe fame.

Slusser, who has written extensively on the history of Ravenscroft and environs, filled in some detail for us. "The hillside to be demolished was the old Reverend Buxton Estate, which also became the North State Fitting School of Thomas Wolfe acclaim," he recounted. "The hill was demolished in 1926 for the Buxton Hill development and was turned into Banks Avenue and Buxton Avenue, now called the South Slope, known for enterprises such as the Green Man Brewery."

Slusser referred to the "Bird's-Eye View of the City of Asheville," which shows the hillside and the Buxton Estate (South Slope) as it appeared in the late 1800s. Southside Avenue is in view in the lower right-hand corner. Buxton's home, which was demolished, was just above the avenue.

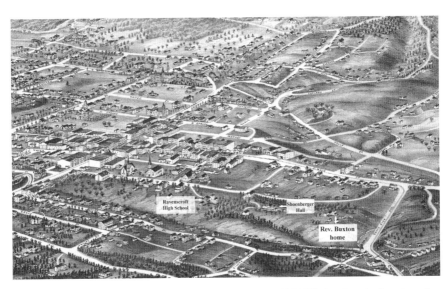

Detail from "Bird's-Eye View of the City of Asheville" (MAP202) showing the location of the Buxton house and Ravenscroft on Buxton Hill. Originally published by Ruger & Stoner, Madison, Wisconsin, with lithograph by Burleigh Lithographing Establishment, Troy, New York. *Map 202 from the North Carolina Collection.*

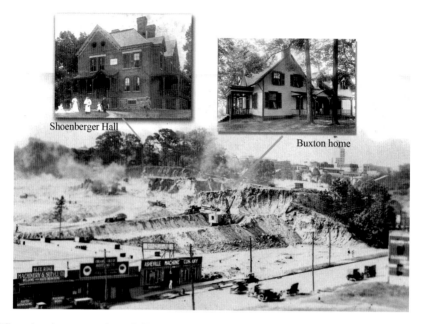

When the photo was enlarged, Shoenberger Hall (*left*; C762-8) was barely visible, and Reverend Buxton's old home (*right*; F741-5) was no longer extant. The hillside where the home had been was leveled.

In the demolition photo above, on the hill and barely visible through trees and clouds of dust, one can see the old Shoenberger Hall, which had been at 60 Ravenscroft Drive. The hall survived the demolition. Slusser says the building to the left of Shoenberger, mostly obscured, was the Arizona Apartment building, which is also visible in the aerial view. He sent us a photo of Shoenberger Hall with a note that "in your photo you can make out the end of the porch on the right end of the building."

Puzzle solved. The demolition in the photo was that of the "hill wooded by magnificent trees" mentioned in Thomas Wolfe's *Look Homeward, Angel*. Slusser describes the hill's history in his book *The Ravenscroft School in Asheville*:

> *During the first half of the twentieth century, while Ravenscroft was being used as a boarding house and in the hands of successive owners and managers, Shoenberger Hall remained in the hands of the* [Episcopal Church's] *Missionary District of Asheville.* [It was the home of Bishop Junius Horner and family and of Reverend A.H. Stubbs.]...*Just south of Shoenberger Hall, though not technically on missionary district land, was Buxton Place, the former home of the Rev. Jarvis Buxton, founder of the*

Ravenscroft schools. The Rev. Buxton's daughter, Mary, had inherited the home following the death of her father in 1902. Not surprisingly, she opened a portion of her home as a boarding house named "Buxton Place." The other portion of the home was leased to the "North State Fitting School."…Thomas Wolfe was not only one of the first students of the school (1912–1916), but he also immortalized it and the nearby Shoenberger Hall in his 1929 novel, Look Homeward, Angel, *when he wrote, "Mr. Leonard had leased an old pre-war house, set on a hill wooded by magnificent trees. It faced west and south, looking toward Biltburn, and abruptly down on South End.*

Slusser goes on to describe the fate of the estate and the hillside:

Unfortunately, the North State Fitting School and Buxton Place did not survive the real-estate frenzy of 1920s Asheville. In 1926, the Buxton Hill Investment Company was organized to develop the Buxton Hill Subdivision on the former site of the Rev. Buxton's property. Not only was the house demolished, but the entire hill was also removed and lowered about 20 feet, leaving a cliff-faced dirt bank along the south property of Shoenberger Hall. [The dirt bank] *remains to this day.*

As it turns out, the *Asheville Citizen* published a similar photograph on January 21, 1926, with the title "Buxton Hill, Old Landmark, To Soon Pass." There is no article to accompany the photo but simply a caption: "Buxton Hill, between Coxe Street on the west, Church Street on the east and Southside on the south, which is now being removed.…Without any advertisement, the entire frontage on the two new streets was sold within a few days' time and before excavation."

Today, the region that was once Buxton Hill is a mix of old-fashioned shops and trendy new businesses. The "cliff-faced dirt bank"—the gash in the hillside that is visible in the demolition photo—is still there and is a backdrop to the parking lot facing Buxton Hall Barbecue, Catawba Brewing Company and Vortex Doughnuts.

On Southside Avenue, where the machine and automotive shops stood, City Transmission Service stands with its whimsical mural of gears.

Most Asheville residents have heard the story of how E.W. Grove removed an entire hill to build his Battery Park Hotel. Until now, few people were aware that an entire hill—and farm and woods—had been removed to create the little South Slope neighborhood. That was the story that was hidden in the photograph at the beginning of this chapter.

Chapter 27

FEBRUARY 1980: THE LEVELING
OF AN ENTIRE CITY BLOCK

In 2016, the North Carolina Room hosted a series of events exploring Asheville in the 1980s—a pivotal decade for the city. Preparing for the first program of the series, on the successful fight to save eleven downtown acres from being demolished to make way for a mall, we delved into what preceded that clash. In fact, right before the Strouse, Greenberg and Co. mid-city mall proposal was announced in March 1980, a full block of 1880s-era historical buildings on Patton Avenue was demolished literally overnight.

This 1960s photo (opposite) shows that block, usually referred to as the Imperial Theater block. It stretched from the Sondley Building at the corner of Patton and Church Streets and included all the buildings down to the Man's Store at the corner of Patton and South Lexington.

Some Asheville residents tried to stop the demolition of this block, but most recall that it happened so quickly it seemed like a done deal. Some who were here at that time say they recall later hearing a theory that the block on Patton was a dry run for how fast the (Strouse-Greenberg) mall area could be torn down.

The buildings were purchased in 1979 by two Asheville banks, Asheville Federal Savings & Loan and the First Citizens Bank & Trust Company. They wanted the property for parking and announced that the old storefronts were in too much disrepair to renovate.

Michael Southern, of Western Representative Archaeology and Historic Preservation, wrote on behalf of the newly established Historical Resources Commission of Asheville to the president of Asheville Federal Savings bank,

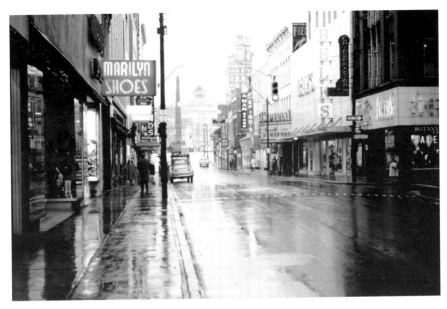

Rainy day view of Patton Avenue between Church and Haywood Streets, looking toward Pack Square, circa 1963–64. Photo by John Basba. *C082-11.*

William Prescott, on November 16, 1979. "Many citizens feel that these building are an integral part of the architectural and historic character of the downtown district, which is listed in the National Register of Historic Places, and that care should be taken to consider every feasible alternative before the structures are removed forever," Southern wrote. He went on to suggest that federal funding was available for historic preservation work, including funds for evaluating costs of rehabilitation.

The Sondley building, built for attorney and historian Foster A. Sondley, was where the author O. Henry kept an office during his stint in Asheville after the turn of the century. Built in 1891 as a four-story building, it was expanded to six stories in 1900. In 1980, it housed J. Pressley Ltd.

Asheville architect and city planner Jim Samsel wrote an editorial that was published on January 1, 1980, in both the morning and evening newspapers, giving harsh criticism to the Asheville Revitalization Committee and the city council for their inaction on the issue: "Both the property owners and the ARC are extremely shortsighted in this action...of the wholesale destruction of an entire block of Patton Avenue for a single-level parking lot. Anymore 'missing teeth' in our streetscape and downtown will end up looking like it needs dentures."

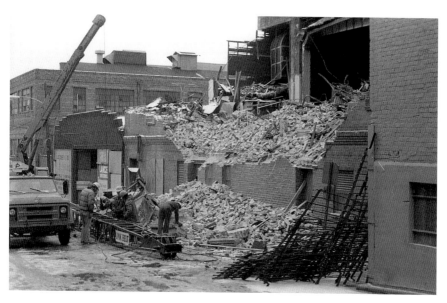

Buildings demolished in the Imperial Theater block, February 1980. *Photo by Peggy Gardner. MS305.001A image 074.*

Bob Terrell also wrote about the demolition of the block in the *Asheville Citizen* in an article titled "Destruction of History." "When the wrecking ball smashes into the Grand Central Annex within the next few days, a lot of history will tumble into rubble," he noted.

Chapter 28

TOURISTS' HOMES: HANGING OUT PLACES

Looking into the area's history of so-called tourist homes, we found they existed longer than we first thought and probably did a lot to help with boarding for tourists. In addition, they most likely provided a good income for women who were willing to work very hard.

The terms "boardinghouse" and "tourist home" are sometimes used interchangeably, though boardinghouse was the term used in early 1900s Asheville city directories. Both terms refer to homes, sometimes expanded for the purpose, to host guests, whether for a day or two or for longer periods of time. Generally, all sections of the home were opened, and meals were taken in a shared dining room.

The tourist home photographs in our collection mostly date to the turn of the nineteenth century, such as the one of Oakhurst, a boardinghouse at 244 East Chestnut Street on the corner of Charlotte Street, seen on the following page. Note the woman in the hat and long dress standing on the front porch and the people on the second-floor porch; Mrs. Ellen V. Glaser was Oakhurst's proprietor.

Boardinghouses were on the rise in the early twentieth century. The 1900 *Asheville City Directory* lists 55 of them, and by 1910, there were 162 listed. In 1902, women owned or managed 55 of them, some 77 percent. Among them was a surprising number of unmarried women.

One fellow from Starkville, Mississippi, found that Mrs. M.E. Alston's boardinghouse, the Chatham, summarized his stay on the back of a postcard sent in 1911. "This is my 'hanging out' place,'" he wrote. "I am

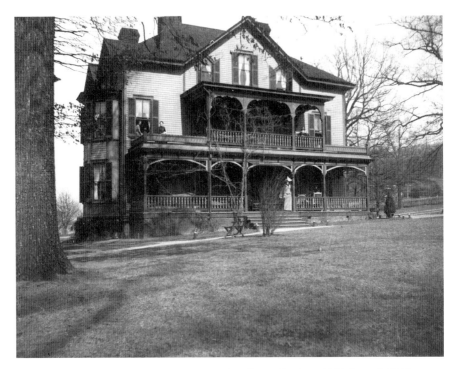

Oakhurst, a boardinghouse that appeared in city directories from 1899 through 1906. It stood at the intersection of East Chestnut and Charlotte Streets in Asheville. Photo is undated. *A523-8.*

not feeling the best in the world but hope you all are. I like the place fine, but consumptives are plentiful....Don't forget my cows if you possibly have the time. Joe."

The most famous Asheville boardinghouse, made so by the proprietor's son, was the Old Kentucky Home. In this 1914 photograph (opposite, bottom), Thomas Wolfe poses with some of the boarders there. Julia Wolfe, Thomas's mother and proprietor of the boarding home, was a good businesswoman. She used the income from her boarding business to further other real estate investments and build more income for the family. Unfortunately, despite her fiscal success, all was lost in the Great Depression.

Moving on into the 1930s, '40s and '50s, the number of boardinghouses seems to have declined, but they were still prevalent and still helped house Asheville's guests. One popular establishment was the Belvedere, at 73 Merrimon Avenue.

Jacqueline A. Ward Britton, a former librarian at Pack Memorial Library, wrote an informative account on the house owned by her family, *Remembering*

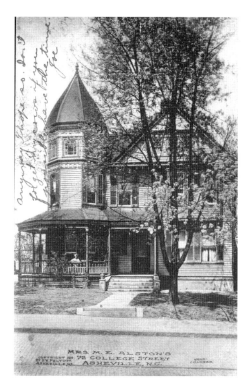

Right: Chatham, a boardinghouse operated by Mrs. M.E. Alston at 72 College Street in Asheville. Copyright 1910 by H.W. Pelton. *AC835*.

Below: Thomas Wolfe with a group of boarders on the side lawn of the Old Kentucky Home. The boardinghouse was operated by his mother, Julia Westall Wolfe. Photograph taken circa 1913–15. *W135-8*.

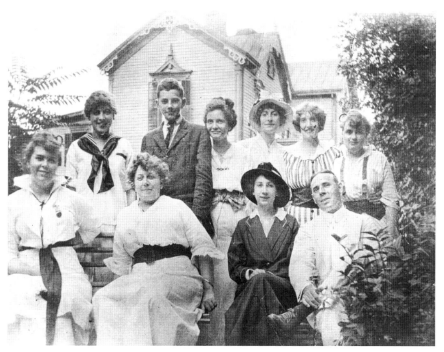

the Belvedere: Celebrating 50 Years of the Ward Family in Asheville, North Carolina, 1949–1999. Britton wrote it in 1999, as her family was selling "one of the last of Asheville's old-style tourist homes." She cited the City of Asheville's "stricter building occupancy codes which made compliance difficult, even with liberal tax credits for restoration work."

Researching the history of the house, Britton found that it was designed by Richard Sharp Smith and built in 1905 for Captain Thomas Johnston, a former mayor of Asheville. When William Henry and Nellie Byers Ward purchased the house in 1949, it was "already functioning as a rooming house with at least six rooms to let, and had recently been named 'The Belvedere.'"

Britton points out that the Belvedere represented an opportunity for an astute woman to support herself and her family. She adds, "There were always some long-term residents; people who either rented by the week while they worked in Asheville and returned home on the weekends, or those who lived there full-time, sometimes until their deaths. But there were always one or two rooms kept available for the more profitable tourist trade."

The Belvedere still stands. Since 2009, it has housed a local business, one that's also known as a "hanging out place": the Secret Spa and Salon.

Chapter 29

GRACE: A COMMUNITY THAT GOT ABSORBED BY AN AVENUE

The loaded questions are when did Grace begin, what area did it include and where did the community get its name? Where was Grace? My best guess is, if you are driving north on Merrimon Avenue, after you top the hill at the intersection of Gracelyn Road, from that point and looking out at the beautiful stretch of land in front of you, especially taking in the mountain view past Grace Episcopal Church, that was the community of Grace. Driving through Grace today, one would scarcely expect to see this assortment of buildings, cars and busy pedestrians spanning the width of Merrimon Avenue.

We have one newspaper article in our clipping files in the North Carolina Room to help point to the history of the community. "Grace Area Taking On a New Face" was published in the *Asheville Times* on July 25, 1973. "Grace was a cluster of stores at the end of the street car tracks. Merrimon was an avenue of fine homes, and Grace was a community way out in the country.…As late as just a few years ago, Grace was an independent community. Civic pride centered around Grace High School athletics. Its football and basketball teams often won the county championships."

Grace High School was built in 1914–15 and torn down in 1960, replaced at the same location with Grace Elementary School, built in 1962. The name changed to Ira B. Jones to honor the principal who had served there since 1931.

The Grace Supply Company was formed in 1918 by Holmes Bryson, Asheville mayor from 1937 to 1941. It was a stock company with Jim

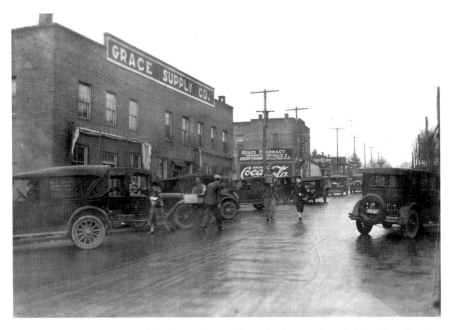

Street view looking south on Merrimon Avenue, from the intersection of Ottari Road and Merrimon Avenue. Circa 1935. *Left to right*: Grace Supply Co., Grace Pharmacy ("Drugs") and Asheville Ice Company depot. *MS285, photo O091-DS.*

McElroy (former county commissioner) and Frank Edwards. It served the community as a grocery, feed, clothing and hardware store and a coal yard. It was a successor to J.E. Johnson and S.K. Green and Co. Grace Supply.

According to Miller's 1931 *Asheville City Directory*, the building was numbered 637–41 Merrimon Avenue. A year later, Merrimon Avenue underwent a new numbering system, giving the building its present address of 853–55 Merrimon Avenue.

In this picture, the Grace Supply Company building is the brick building near the center of the photo. On the left is a Standard Oil service station. Standard Oil Company stations later became Esso and then Exxon. The filling station at 873 Merrimon was listed as a Standard Oil Company station until the 1940s, when it became Ford's Esso station (Norman E. Ford). An Exxon station stood at that location until 2017, when it was razed.

As early as 1930, Grace residents did not have to take the two-mile trip over the hill into Asheville in order to shop for most necessities. There in their own little valley, on Merrimon Avenue, they had pharmacies, department stores, cabinetmakers and several gas stations. Miller's city directory lists the

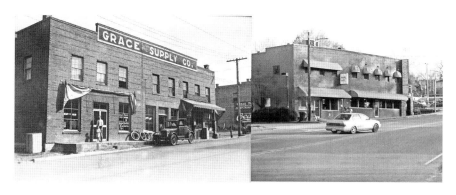

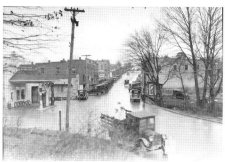
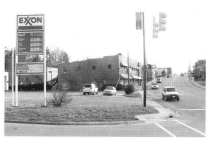

Top: View of the Grace Supply building circa 1935 and as it looks today. *MS285, photo O093-DS.*

Bottom: Looking south on Merrimon Avenue from the intersection of Ottari Road and Merrimon, circa 1935, with the same intersection as it looks today. *MS285, photo O077-DS.*

following addresses on Merrimon Avenue, beginning at Ottari Road and traveling uphill to Gracelyn Road:

- 873 Standard Oil Company service station, at the bottom of the hill across from Grace Episcopal Church
- 861 The Furniture Shop (in 1940, listed as Raleigh Kilpatrick, cabinetmaker)
- 857 Grace Dry Goods Company
- 853–55 Grace Supply, Inc., general merchandise
- 841 Grace Pharmacy
- 837 Asheville Ice Company

At the corner of Clairmont Avenue was the A&P grocer, and at the top of the hill, on the left, was Cline's Pharmacy at 793 Merrimon. Also known as

Hester's Pharmacy and Beaver Lake Pharmacy, the building stands today. It is the old building with "Robinson 1927" at the top.

Some of you may recall Citizen's Hardware in the lot now housing Walgreens Pharmacy. I hadn't realized Citizen's was a local business. It was formed in 1941 by Thomas Arthur Groce Jr. and was located in what had been the Grace Pharmacy building at 841 Merrimon.

The 1973 newspaper article said, "Anyone who's been away from Grace the last few years wouldn't recognize it now. Not a landmark remains in the area, except the present café building and the soon-to-be torn down Citizen's Hardware Building." That would have been the building in the below photo. A second Citizens building had been built in 1973, set back farther from the street. The business was sold by Thomas Groce's son Jim to new owners Max and Beverly Corte in 1998, and the 1973 building was razed recently for the construction of Walgreens.

Regarding when the community came to be called Grace and why, the post office at Grace was established on November 9, 1889, and Charles B.

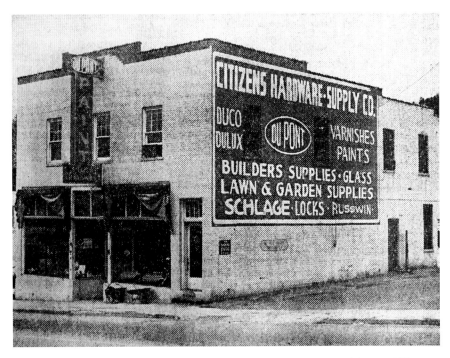

Exterior of Citizens Hardware & Supply Co. on its nineteenth birthday, July 17, 1960. Located at 941 Merrimon Avenue. *Slide from MS116 Robert Fortune Collection, "History of Asheville" slide series.*

Way was the postmaster. This was the earliest found date for the area's name, as well as proof that the community was not named for the first postmaster, as some communities were.

A good guess would be that the community was named after Grace Mission, the early mission established by Trinity Episcopal, which became Grace Episcopal Church. But the church's history says that the mission "began in 1867 with the construction of a log chapel known as Beaverdam Mission. By the 1880s, the mission had taken on the name of the little community in which it was located, Grace." A history of the church published in 1967, and quoting a history written by Miss Fannie Patton, says that "it is around 1889 that the name 'Grace Mission,' or 'Grace Chapel,' comes to be used consistently, having replaced the earlier designation of 'Beaver Dam Mission,' Grace being the name of the steadily growing community in which the mission church was and is located."

In *Beaverdam: Historic Valley of the Blue Ridge Mountains*, Rex Redmon writes, "We searched diligently to find the source of the name, feeling sure it was associated in some way with His Grace the Bishop Francis Asbury." Asbury traveled to this area to preach in 1800 and stayed at the Killian home, still in existence on Beaverdam Road. That's a long stretch of time between 1800 and 1889, but some locals speculate that remnants of his visit might have given cause for the name of Grace.

"Grace, RFD 1, Buncombe County" was the listing for this quiet community in the 1920 city directory. Though the origins of the name remain a mystery, thanks to these newfound photographs, a view of this thriving neighborhood as it was eighty years ago is no longer hidden.

Chapter 30

CAMP DELLWOOD

A lovely spot among the hills,
A sky of blue above,
And trees that bend in graceful form,
These make the camp I love.
—Mary Mitchell Westall

C amp Dellwood, established in the 1920s, afforded girls ages nine to nineteen a summer filled with outdoor sports, arts and crafts, socializing and fun. Under the direction of Mr. and Mrs. George Mason Swift, it was located near Lake Junaluska in Haywood County. Among its enthusiastic campers was Mary Mitchell Westall of Asheville, whose love of camp life is well documented in her poetry, journal, photograph album, autograph books, camp logs and other camp publications. A study of these materials provides a complete picture of camp life during that period (1928–33).

The camp was constructed on the slope of a mountain at 3,200 feet elevation, "insuring delightful days and cool nights," a pamphlet boasted in 1929. It consisted of a lodge for group activities, a dining hall and kitchen, a craft building and a nature den. The campers' cabins, called kiosks, were lit with electricity. Modern plumbing with hot and cold showers was provided, along with "a splendid cuisine to assure the health and comfort of the girls."

The Camp Dellwood publication sent to prospective campers specified the items of clothing each girl should bring. For sports, two pairs of blue

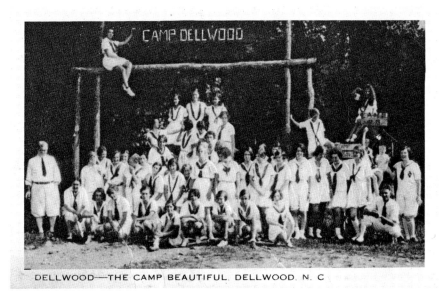

DELLWOOD—THE CAMP BEAUTIFUL, DELLWOOD, N. C

Postcard for Camp Dellwood, circa 1930. *MS294.001E, photo A.*

bloomers were required, while two pairs of white twill bloomers were needed for dress wear. White middy blouses, scarlet middy ties and a red sweater complemented both. To ensure uniformity, these were ordered from the camp's official outfitter, M.V. Moore in Asheville. Also on the supply list: a wool bathing suit, eight pairs of socks, dark woolen blankets, a flashlight and a Bible.

A spirit of friendly rivalry was encouraged among campers, who were divided into two teams named the Speedies and the Swifties. They competed in archery, basketball, track, canoeing, tennis, hiking, swimming and canoeing on the lake. Horseback riding was also featured as the girls learned to sit, post and give signals correctly while riding along mountain trails. The season culminated with the final horse show, described in the camp publication as "one of the most popular events of the camp season."

In addition to sports, campers stayed busy with craft projects, interpretive dancing, tap dancing, dramatics and nature study. Campfire meetings were held for singing and storytelling and to give the leaders a chance to speak. "Tonight we had a pajama party in the lodge," Westall wrote in her journal on July 15, 1930. "I hope that everyone is getting as much out of camp as I feel I am and that they love it as much."

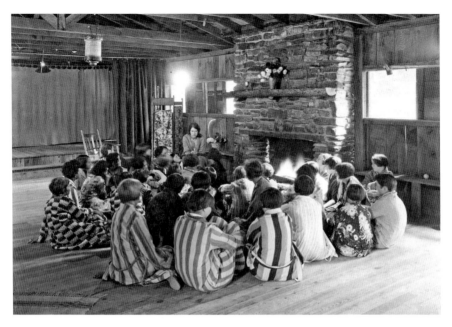

Above: Photograph of a pajama party in the lodge that appeared in the Camp Dellwood publication sent to prospective campers, 1929. *MS294 5-006. MS294.001E, photo B.*

Opposite: Snapshot of Dellwood campers having fun in Mary Mitchell Westall's photograph album, 1928–30. *MS294.001E, photo C.*

A listing of "Happy Days" in the camp publication testifies that the camp calendar was filled with special events intended to make camp life exciting. Those included barbecues, camp-outs, a beach party, vaudeville night, Christmas in July and the Dellwood Prom. Walpurgis Night, held near the end of the summer session, was a highlight. Costumed campers portrayed Peter Pan, fairy queens, witches, brownies and other characters, dancing and play-acting in a carnival atmosphere. Parents were invited to watch the pageantry. Mary Mitchell Westall described the excitement of the rehearsals, the costumes and the guests' arrivals. Of the production, she wrote, "It went over big. The audience seemed to enjoy it immensely." A photomontage appeared in the Camp Dellwood publication sent to prospective campers.

Summer camp is all about fun and friends, "like a lovely big family," wrote Westall. "It certainly is fine to be in a place so beautiful and to know such girls. I just know I will never forget my first real friends." Her autograph books also testify to the importance of friendship among campers, many of whom returned to Camp Dellwood year after year. Photos such as these from her album show the jokes and hijinks that filled their days.

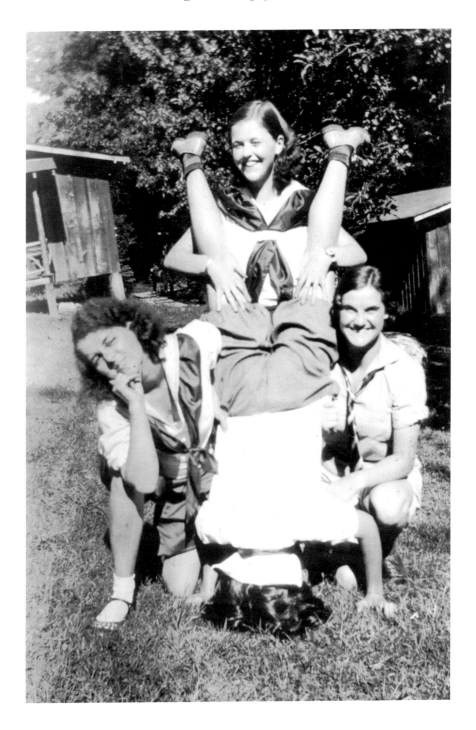

Westall was compelled to pen poetic tributes to the camp, including this one:

Because it is a lovely place
With friends so kind and good,
Because it gives me all things fine,
I love dear Camp Dellwood.

Chapter 31

CATHOLIC EDUCATION IN ASHEVILLE

Asheville once had a flourishing system of parochial primary and secondary schools. Catholic schools reached their peak in both number and enrollment in the 1950s and '60s before making a quick retreat in the '70s. A decline in religious vocations greatly reduced the availability of nuns and priests to staff the schools, and the economics of hiring lay teachers to fill classroom vacancies accelerated their demise.

The oldest and best known of the local Catholic schools was St. Genevieve of the Pines, which at one time occupied a twenty-six-acre tract on Victoria Road. By the 1960s, St. Genevieve's incorporated four distinct boarding and day schools on its campus, including the School for Secretaries, a grammar and high school for girls and Gibbons Hall School for Boys. St. Genevieve's high school graduated its last class in 1972, and St. Genevieve–Gibbons Hall day school ultimately merged with Asheville Country Day School, now known as Carolina Day School, in 1987. St. Genevieve's was unique in that it was not a diocesan school; instead, it was operated by the nuns of an institute called the Religious of Christian Education. Noted novelist Gail Godwin is a St. Genevieve's graduate.

Asheville Catholic High School originated as St. Francis School for Boys in 1949 and was run by Franciscan friars. The school became co-ed in 1957, grew steadily to an enrollment of approximately 150 day students in the 1960s and closed due to a sharp decline in enrollment in 1972. Residents of the pre-seminary St. John Vianney Hall attended classes at Asheville Catholic High School. As was the case with the nearby St. Genevieve's

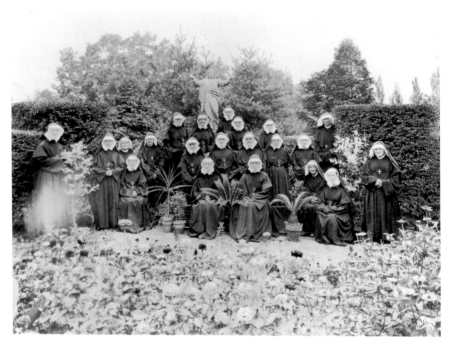

Group portrait showing twenty-one nuns from St. Genevieve's. Photo by H.W. Pelton, 1935. *J103-8.*

campus, the Asheville Catholic campus was sold to Asheville-Buncombe Technical Community College in the mid-'70s. A-B Tech's Laurel Building, gymnasium and the Smith-McDowell House were all once part of the Asheville Catholic campus.

Cannongate, a Catholic high school not affiliated with the Diocese of Charlotte, opened in Fletcher in 2013 and is presently the only Catholic high school west of Charlotte.

Three primary schools attached to parishes also operated here. St. Joan of Arc and St. Eugene Catholic School were attached to their respective parishes. St. Joan of Arc School, built in 1950, was on Haywood Road in West Asheville, and St. Eugene's opened in 1955 on Culvern Street, just off Beaverdam Road in North Asheville. The two schools merged in 1980 to form Asheville Catholic School, which continues to operate on the former St. Eugene's campus. The St. Joan of Arc campus was sold for commercial development, and the church itself relocated to Candler in 2007.

St. Anthony of Padua School, which was opened by the Franciscans in 1936 on Walton Street in the Southside neighborhood, closed in 1969.

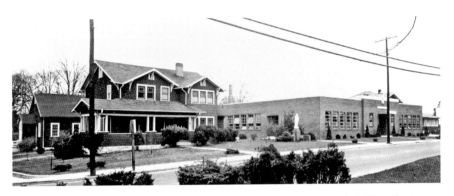

St. Joan of Arc School at 915 Haywood Road in West Asheville, circa 1940. The Gardner House (*at right in background*) was the original building when the school was established, circa 1928. *B705-8.*

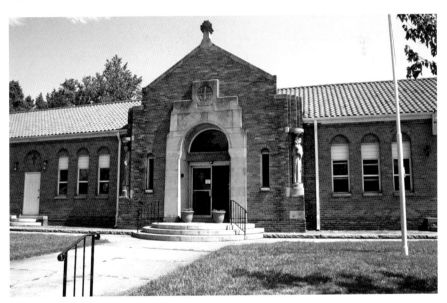

St. Anthony's School, operated by Catholic nuns to serve African American students in grades one through eight during the years 1936 to 1968. Photo by Richard Hansley. *RHC-136-DS image 1.*

It had served primarily African American students; henceforth, the local Catholic schools were integrated.

Ed Sheary, retired director of Buncombe County Public Libraries, is a 1967 graduate of St. Eugene's School and a 1971 graduate of Asheville Catholic High School.

Chapter 32

MARGARET'S SUPPER CLUB
AND BROWN BAGGING *and*
A SMITH & CARRIER BUILDING
AND THE WRECKING BALL

A patron told us one day that his parents' favorite spot for dinner and dancing was Margaret's Supper Club on the Weaverville Highway. He also educated us on the previous practice of "brown bagging." Prior to 1979, when Asheville enacted a liquor-by-the-drink law, his parents used to brown bag. They would take their liquor (in a bag) to a restaurant, and the wait staff would serve it.

Margaret's Supper Club was run by Margaret Fleming. After ten years of operating the Lantern Grill on Beaverdam Road and then in the old Governor Craig residence on Black Mountain Highway, she opened the eatery first at 72 Broadway in downtown Asheville. A main specialty there was "a real steak dinner—the steak cooked just right and all the best trimmings," according to a September 16, 1935 report in the *Asheville Citizen*. Fleming's pride was her Southern Fried Chicken dinner, which, she said, "was the best in the whole South."

In 1940, Fleming moved the restaurant to Weaverville Highway, just past Beaver Lake. She was fined twenty-five dollars in 1938 for violating the liquor laws when "about a case of whisky was confiscated in a raid at the dine and dance place," the *Asheville Citizen* reported. Several other fines and the loss of a beer license followed; the same occurred at Emma Adler's Sky Club and Russell McKenzie's Chez Paul restaurant, the newspaper reported in August 1957.

In March 2016, *Asheville Citizen-Times* columnist Carole Currie wrote that her "father warned her never to go to Chez Paul or the Sky Club because both sold mixed drinks illegally and they were regularly raided." She went to Chez Paul anyway, shortly after getting married, because there was a dance band and they had good steaks.

Margaret's claimed to be "Asheville's oldest Supper Club," dating back to 1929. It closed in 1975 after the death of Fleming's husband. Then a resident of the Vanderbilt Apartments and a member of St. Mary's Episcopal Church, Margaret died in 1981.

Two stories in one! We love rabbit holes as much as anyone, and Margaret's Supper Club led us to a pretty good find. The rabbit hole was the Supper Club's original downtown location at 72 Broadway. We had no building information for that address, although it would have been beside the majestic Masonic Lodge at 80 Broadway. The Lodge was designed by Smith & Carrier, the company that designed all the fraternal organizations in Asheville, including the Elks House, Eagles Home and the Asheville Club.

An Internet search led to a photograph in the E.M. Ball Collection in UNCA's Special Collections. It is identified as the "Ambler home, later American Legion Home on Broadway," and has the description: "Home of Dr. Arthur Ambler, physician of Ambler Heights Sanitarium. Brick."

A first look at the building could easily place it on the Biltmore Estate, perhaps part of the farm and stables. In further searching for Ambler's home, we found an article in the *Citizen* on June 28, 1921, announcing that Dr. Arthur C. Ambler would be maintaining his offices of general practice of medicine in the building occupied by his father, Dr. Chase P. Ambler.

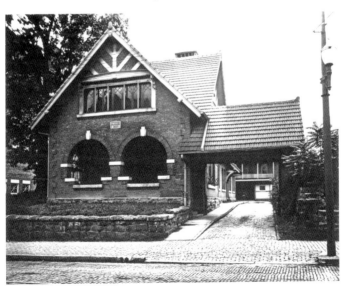

Photograph of Dr. Arthur C. Ambler's office at 72 Broadway designed by Richard Sharp Smith, used with permission from UNCA Special Collections. *B1815.*

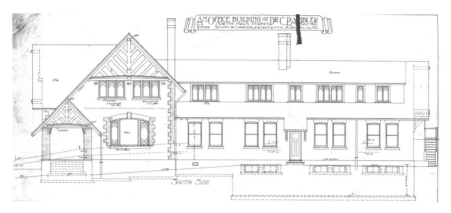

Architectural drawing titled "An Office Building for Dr. C.P. Ambler—North Main Street—South Side. 1910–05." Used with permission from the Asheville Art Museum. *RS0685.1.*

And that led to the building's architectural drawings that are in our North Carolina Room collection. The plans were drawn by none other than Smith & Carrier. Richard Sharp Smith and Albert Heath Carrier were in business together from 1906 until Smith's death in 1924. R.S. Smith, of course, was superintending architect at the Biltmore Estate.

The building was sold to the Kiffin Rockwell post of the American Legion in 1940 to be used as its assembly hall. As time went on, the American Legion post's members dwindled, and they put the building up for sale in 1948. The building's tile roof was noted, as well as an adjoining 50-by-150-foot vacant lot. No offers were accepted.

That is until 1957, when the City of Asheville made an offer. According to an article in the *Citizen-Times* on January 9, 1957, the city would demolish the building and operate a parking lot on the property, and the post would lease it from the city, with the city giving back 45 percent of parking proceeds. The site would "be the first off-street municipal parking lot on Broadway."

One last article told of the fate of the Ambler building. An ad was placed in the *Asheville Citizen-Times* on May 12, 1957, and it was horrifying! "WRECKING AMERICAN LEGION BUILDING—Finest doors, flooring, framing and brick—offered for sale in many years. Most beautiful tile roof in Asheville. See L.D. Jenkins on job. 72 Broadway."

Chapter 33

ORA STREET CHURCH

When we learned of a long-standing but now-shuttered Asheville church, Ora Street Presbyterian, we were curious to learn and document its unique history.

A 1910 photo postcard by Luther Higgason (seen on the following page) introduced us to the Reverend Edwin Lysander Grau, who briefly helmed the church. He was born in 1864 in Lancaster, Pennsylvania, and first appeared in the 1909 *Asheville City Directory*, identified as a boarder at 96 Bartlett Street. He likely arrived in Asheville sometime in 1908. At that time, he preached at Depot Presbyterian Church, located at 94 Ora Street. Grau was engaged in October 1908 to the former Mary Frances Trompeter, who was born in Louisville, Kentucky, in 1890.

According to information from the Buncombe County Register of Deeds, Grau purchased a lot on Ora Street in October 1908. The street runs from Bartlett Street to Ralph Street, roughly parallel to South French Broad Avenue. Grau and his new bride probably built the house on the lot, which became #37. It's still occupied today. The Graus' daughter, Mary Frances, was born on May 11, 1910. According to the writing on the back of the postcard, the photograph was taken sometime in June of that year.

The photo postcard was addressed to "My Faithful Elder/J.H. Gudger," who was an elder of the church. He and his wife, Sue, lived at 30 Ora Street. Gudger was a freight conductor for the Southern Railway. In 1922, the couple built an eight-room home at 345 South French Broad. The Grau family sold their home in 1911 and moved to Trenton, Tennessee.

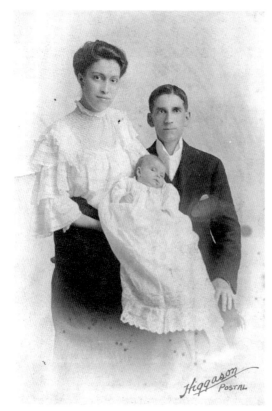

Left: Postcard portrait of the Reverend and Mrs. E.L. Grau, the first pastor of Ora Street Presbyterian Church, with two-month-old baby Mary Frances Grau, born May 11, 1910. *AE182*.

Below: Reverend Grau and his new bride probably built the house on the lot, which became #37. It's still occupied today. *Photo by Terry Taylor, 2017.*

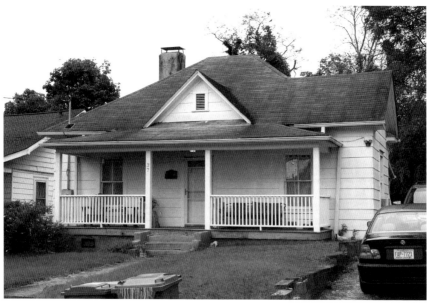

Ora Street Presbyterian had several other ministers until 1936, when it became the First Church of the Nazarene. In 1950, it became Ora Community Chapel Church of God and, in 1955, Ora Street Church of God. It retained that name for fifty years, until it was sold to a holding company in 2014. Through the years, the church building was variously listed as either #94 or #96. Here's a photo of Ora Street Church of God taken in the 1980s.

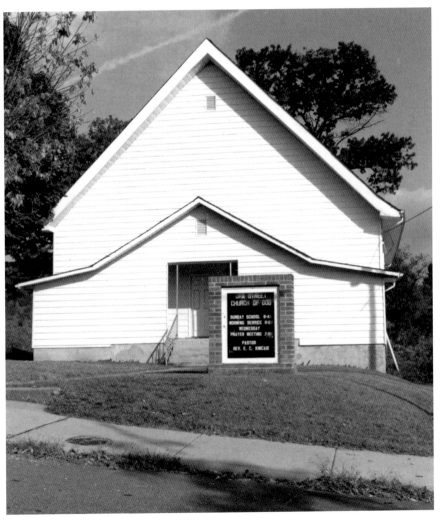

Photo of Ora Street Church of God, a simple white frame church with no windows on the entrance side. From a scrapbook titled "Asheville's Black Churches." The album was made in 1980 by Gladys C. Kennedy; color photographs were taken by John Davis. *MS163, photo K850-4.*

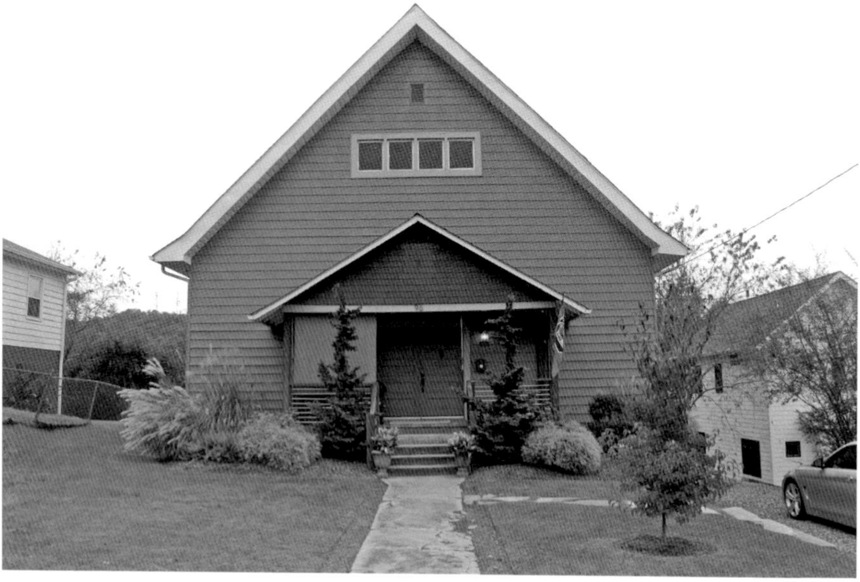

The renovated Ora Street Church building is now a family home. The double door is painted a welcoming red. *Photo by Terry Taylor, 2017.*

And here is the renovated building, which is now a family home with the double door painted a welcoming red.

PART VI

Immigrants Find a Home

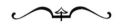

Chapter 34

THE PEARLMAN FAMILY: THREE GENERATIONS OF SELLING FURNITURE

Brothers Marvin "Skip" and Lowell R. Pearlman came to us in 2013 with their family collection. A large collection, it was one of our first collections documenting Jewish residents. Skip Pearlman has given many talks locally to keep his ancestors' past and their work alive. He participated in our local history program on Jewish businesses and was on one of the panels for our 1980s series. We are proud to house the Pearlman family archives. Asheville was a destination for many immigrant families that flourished and added to the uniqueness of the community and enrichment of the town.

In 1889, six brothers and three sisters left a small village in Lithuania, Russia. One girl and four brothers came to Asheville. The Michalove brothers were Solomon H., Isaac, Louis and Abe, and their sister was Anna Michalove Swartzberg. To earn a living, they "first peddled in the countryside on foot, on horseback, and from wagons. As their situation improved, the brothers established small stores and sold their wares from them," the *Asheville Citizen-Times* recorded in a September 2, 1982 retrospective. By 1896, S.H. and Abe had launched the IXL grocery, first at 41 College Street. It became "an Asheville institution known for its fine china, glass, and silver," the newspaper noted.

Isaac (born in 1858) and his wife, Sarah Malke Michalove (born in 1854), first opened their own grocery at the corner of Valley and Eagle Streets. Then they operated the Michalove Wholesale Grocery Company. Isaac applied for his U.S. citizenship, along with five other foreign-born Asheville residents, at the Federal Building in September 1915.

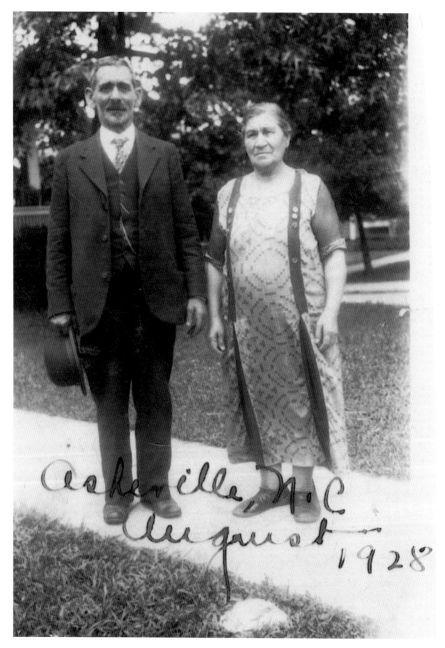

Isaac and Sarah Malke Michalove, Asheville, 1928. *MS239.002A photo A.*

Isaac died in Asheville in 1935 after having lived here for forty-five years. Sarah died in Asheville in 1944. Isaac and Sarah's daughter Hattie, born on September 20, 1890, married Barney Pearlman, whose family immigrated to the United States in 1901 and came to Asheville in 1908.

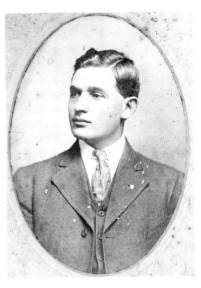

Barney operated several groceries in Asheville and worked for a time at his uncle's IXL store before opening his own small store, Railroad Salvage Company, on Patton Avenue, in late 1927. Barney was a salvage agent for the Southern Railway, and he featured refused, lost and unclaimed furniture, groceries, plumbing fixtures and stoves—just about anything the railroad carried. Barney's son Fred Pearlman later said, "We were the forerunners of the discount houses in Asheville."

Studio portrait of Barney Pearlman, Asheville, North Carolina. Barney was born in 1895, making the photo circa 1920. *MS239.001A photo C.*

A substantial part of the business's sales came from bulk groceries like flour, sugar, salt, lard, rice and oats—that is, until the day a man walked into the store and engaged Barney and Hattie in conversation. He introduced himself as Mr. J.E. Broyhill from Lenoir and asked them if they might be interested in selling furniture. Broyhill said he and his brothers were making furniture in Lenoir and had a small business there, the Lenoir Chair Company. They were in the sawmill business and had started manufacturing some basic finished wood furniture.

Barney told Broyhill they would most certainly like to sell furniture, but unfortunately, they did not have sufficient cash funds to purchase any inventory. (This was in the beginning of the Great Depression.) Broyhill told them he would consign them some furniture and would then stop by every couple of weeks and collect the money on items sold. That's how the Pearlmans got into the furniture business. The Pearlmans remained lifelong friends and customers of the Broyhill Furniture Company.

The Railroad Salvage Store became Pearlman's Railroad Salvage when it moved in 1930 to larger headquarters in what had been the Haywood Garage at 38–58 Haywood Street, also referred to as the Haywood Building,

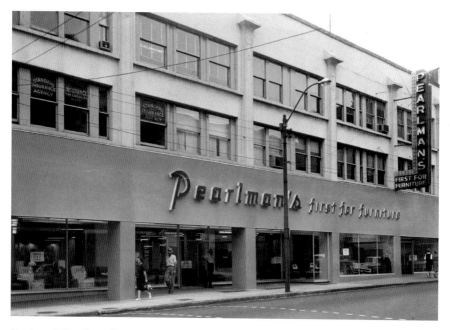

Pearlman's Furniture Store, 56 Haywood Street, as it appeared in the 1960s. Photo by Juanita Wilson. *E862-DS.*

built in 1917 by Paul Roebling. It was the first major commercial building on Haywood Street. Remodeling the former garage included providing a new entrance, adding a new storefront with two large show windows and providing a rear entrance.

In 1940, the Pearlmans also built the Pearlman building on Page Avenue, which connected through the back of their Haywood Street store. The Page Avenue location was the first in the area to carry discounted furniture.

The Pearlman company expanded to other towns after World War II, from Charlotte west to Waynesville. The Pearlman Company did many good things for the Asheville community, including starting the Pearlman Family Scholarship for students from Asheville's black high school, Stephens-Lee.

The Asheville store moved to Tunnel Road across from the Asheville Mall in November 1973. Fred Pearlman's two sons, Marvin "Skip" and Lowell Pearlman, became the third generation to operate the store.

Pearlman's downtown locations were closed Sundays and on the Jewish holidays Rosh Hashanah and Yom Kippur. But when the business moved to 246 Tunnel Road, across from the Asheville Mall, that changed. As Skip Pearlman said, "Sunday openings had become commonplace as many businesses left downtown Asheville. I personally had a more secular approach to being observant." The bottom line was, "We stayed open on Sundays and Jewish holidays."

Pearlman's Furniture store closed in 1996, ending a sixty-nine-year run as an Asheville family-owned business. In 2002, Skip and Mary Hood Pearlman donated the sixty-thousand-square-foot building at 30 Meadow Road to Habitat for Humanity for its new home store, which remains there today.

Chapter 35

AMERICANIZATION CLASSES
AT THE GROVE PARK INN

Have you identified and labeled your family photo albums with dates and names? Most people don't. You can imagine the value an archivist or a historian places on well-documented photographs. One of the best identified collections we have came from the work of the Buncombe County School for Adults program begun in 1918 by Elizabeth C. Morriss and her teachers. They worked in all areas of Buncombe County to help adults learn to read, including giving lessons on railroad trains. Each of the photos has the name of the person, the place, year and which teacher's class they were in. We have two different collections documenting the literacy program. One mostly documents people from the Sandy Mush and Turkey Greek sections and dates from 1922 to 1941. The other collection we received from the Buncombe County Schools Administration archives, and it covers sections all over the county, including Americanization classes held at the Grove Park Inn for recent immigrants to this area.

The Buncombe County Community (Night) School's literacy program was a forerunner in the state to help teach literacy to adults, particularly in rural communities. From 1917 to 1920, the program taught over three thousand adults to read and write, and it continued for many years thereafter.

A not-as-well-known part of the school's program was the Americanization classes, where English was taught to non-English speakers. In the early 1920s, Asheville was home to immigrants from Italy, Russia, Greece, Romania, France and Poland. Americanization classes were held in the Orange Street School and, interestingly enough, also at the Grove Park Inn, where many of the students were employed as chefs and grounds workers.

This photograph (opposite, top) shows a teacher, Mrs. Knight, with three of her pupils, all Italian cooks at Grove Park Inn, in the mid-1920s.

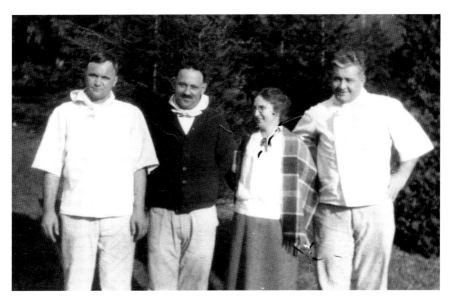

Mrs. Knight with three of her students, all of whom were Italian cooks at the Grove Park Inn, circa 1924–25. *Left to right*: Pasgreale Moschio, Lugi Cantarella and John Cantarella; the latter two are likely chefs. The Cantarella family came from Morasco, Italy. Photo by H.W. Pelton. *MS247.002G photo O.*

According to his naturalization papers, Ferucio Paganin was born in 1894 in Taibon (Agordino), Italy, and came to Asheville at the age of thirty-one, leaving his wife behind.

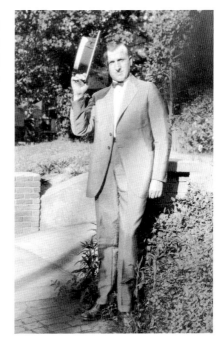

Italian stonemason Ferucio Paganin poses for the photographer, circa 1924–25. Photo by H.W. Pelton. *MS247.002G photo S.*

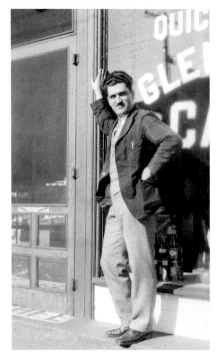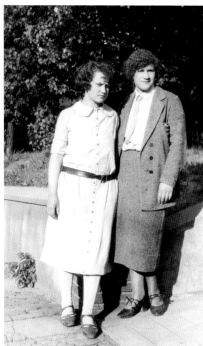

Left: James Klomenous Karembelas, the Greek proprietor of the Glen Rock Café, stands in front of his Depot Street café, 1925. Photo by H.W. Pelton. *MS247.002G photo R.*

Right: Italians Emma Solary (*right*) and daughter Jean pose together, 1925. Photo by H.W. Pelton. *MS247.002G photo X.*

James Klomenous Karembelas, pictured above in 1925, was born in 1899 and came here from Sparta, Greece. He is listed in the 1926 *Asheville City Directory* as the proprietor of the Glen Rock Café, located across from the Railroad Depot.

Speranza Solary, a widow, immigrated in 1903 from Pesares, Italy, with her husband, John, and her children (one son and three daughters). Her daughter Emma is shown here on the left. Her son Leno, a stonemason, "supervised the stone and brick work for Lee Edwards High School (former name of Asheville High School designed by Douglas Ellington) and the Chapel Tower of Duke University and personally did the stone work on the Governor's Western Residence." John Solary died here in 1922; Speranza, a member of St. Lawrence Catholic Church, died in Asheville in 1958 at the age of eighty-one; and Leno died in Asheville in 1968 at the age of sixty-seven.

Chapter 36

THE SAD STORY OF HOP WO, THE CHINESE LAUNDRYMAN

Scrolling through the microfilm one day, we came across a small but eye-catching notice in the July 26, 1894 *Asheville Daily Citizen*: "Chinatown's inhabitants are delighted over the return of Hop Wo, the laundryman, after an absence of several years. Hop Wo has been, since leaving here, in New York, Chicago and Cincinnati and lately in Johnson City, Tenn."

We blinked and read it again. "Chinatown's inhabitants…Asheville?" Chinatown in Asheville was news to all of us. We pursued it a little and found Hop Wo listed in the 1887 *Asheville City Directory* with the location "under 19 S. Main, bds. same." Then we found the name of one Lee Sing. Searching Ancestry.com for anyone living in Asheville in 1880 who was born in China, we found no one.

We surmised that, at best, the newspaper was speaking tongue-in-cheek—hinting that Asheville's "Chinatown" had just a few inhabitants— so we suspended our search.

Then, as luck would have it, during research on another topic, we stumbled across this headline from November 26, 1896, in the *Asheville Citizen-Times*, two years after the first Hop Wo reference we had seen earlier: "Chinatown's Talk: Hop Wo's Laundry Closed, While Hop Takes a Walk."

"Chinatown is agog over the disappearance from the city of one of their number," the article began. "The absent one is Hop Wo, or as the name is Anglicized, Lee Johnson." It was thought that, as he "had become pretty well fixed he had returned to China to enjoy his wealth."

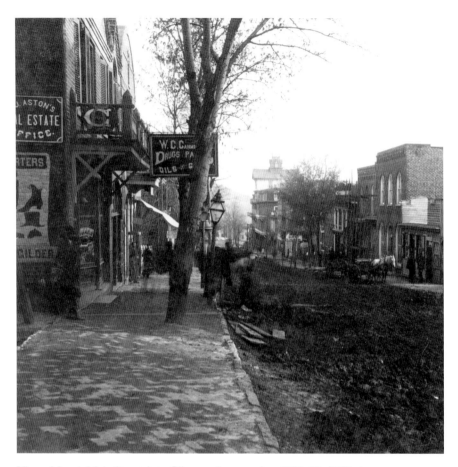

View of South Main Street, later Biltmore Avenue, circa 1883–89. *B520-4.*

As it turns out, the earliest ad for Hop Wo's laundry was in the *Asheville Advance* on June 12, 1886—eight years before the first ad we'd found. Further articles mention other Chinese in Asheville, including Hop Wo's brother, George Wo. Ling Gun had come to Asheville from New York but did not stay long and left here for Morristown, Tennessee, but was assaulted and badly hurt. As the *Asheville Weekly Citizen* of November 16, 1893, reported, "James Johnson, a colored man employed in the laundry here, and who knew Ling Gun, went to Paint Rock to find him and bring him back."

A subsequent newspaper discovery published thirteen years after Hop Wo had left Asheville told us much more. A February 6, 1909, article in the *Asheville Citizen* headlined "Chinese Laundry Is Latest Industrial Project for City" made mention of another Chinese man, Hop Sing, from Cincinnati, who had announced his intention to open a laundry. "After long years of immunity," the article continued, "Asheville is to have a real Chinese laundry."

And then, the long tale of Hop Wo was recounted, beginning with this dire heading: "Tragic End of the First One." According to the newspaper, upon his departure in 1896, Wo boarded a train here without a ticket to begin his visit to his native land, but having limited English skills, he wasn't able to explain himself and was put off the train somewhere near the Tennessee line. "On the second day of his wanderings he stumbled on the cabin of a mountaineer where a woman and a daughter were the only occupants, the husband being at work some distance from the house.... Merely stopping to ask directions, the strange tongue and the still stranger face of the Mongolian filled the woman with terror, and piercing screams rent the air."

Wo's body was found several days later by a search party. This sad tale ended in international complications, with the United States government having to "make a payment of a heavy indemnity to the Chinese government, for the benefit of the dead Chinaman's family," the newspaper reported, adding that the incident had kept Chinese people from coming to this area for many years.

Just what Chinatown looked like in Asheville over 130 years ago, and how many inhabitants it had, remains to be discovered.

Chapter 37

Yutaka Minakuchi: A Story in a Name

One of the delights of cataloguing incoming materials in the North Carolina Room is that the smallest detail can lead down a rabbit hole into worlds of stories. Recently, while working with papers of Albert Heath Carrier, an architect with the firm Smith & Carrier which helped design many of Asheville's historic buildings, we discovered an amazing story from a single name: Yutaka Minakuchi.

Minakuchi, we learned, bought property from Carrier in the early 1900s and worked with him on developing a U.S. version of a Japanese poetry-matching card game, Hyaku-Nin-Shi (Hyakunin Isshu Karuta), that was to be called Bibliquote. Included in the North Carolina Collection is a copy of their agreement that Carrier would fund the printing of the first thousand games for $150. Sadly, we have found no other information on the fate of their initiative.

What else do we know of Minakuchi? According to Asheville city directories of the time, he worked as secretary-treasurer of the Asheville Pepsi-Cola Bottling Company and lived at 77 Montford Avenue with his wife, Olivia (née Buckner). According to Dr. Joseph D. Robinson, Carrier's grandson, who donated the Carrier materials, Smith & Carrier designed this house for Minakuchi.

We learned more from the late Vachel Lindsay, a celebrity poet of the early 1900s, who made a walking tour of the Southeast and stopped at the Minakuchi home. Lindsay recounted the visit in his book *A Handy Guide for Beggars*: "I looked up a scholar from Yale, Yutaka Minakuchi, friend of old

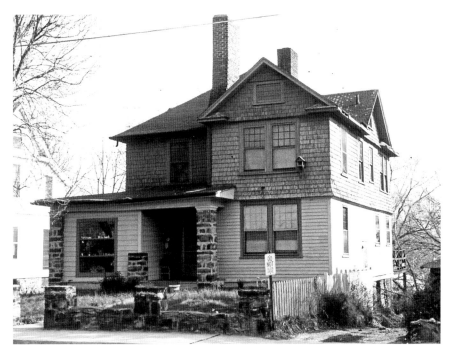

A photo taken from a 1990 survey of deteriorating and dilapidated houses in Montford, this house at 77 Montford Avenue has since been renovated. *MS274.001ZK.*

friends, student of philosophy, in which he instructed me much, first lending me a collar. He became my host in Asheville. It needs no words of mine to enhance the fame of Japanese hospitality."

Minakuchi was born in 1875 in Japan but moved to the United States, where he graduated from the University of North Carolina at Chapel Hill with bachelor's and master's degrees. He also attended Oberlin Theological School and Yale University before becoming a missionary, writer and orator who spoke as part of the Chautauqua Circuit. In his Chautauqua bio and lecture listing (circa 1916), it says he "served an American congregation in Asheville, N.C., for three years as its pastor" and that his lectures covered everything from Japanese culture to ecumenical studies of Eastern and Western religions and American-Japanese relations.

Minakuchi eventually left Asheville for more northern climes. At some point, he divorced Olivia and married Nellie Cook of Vermont, settling in Peacham, Vermont. There, he became pastor of the Congregational church in 1929, remaining until 1938. He then moved to Glover, the birthplace of his wife, where he became a respected community member and continued to lecture.

In 1942, however, the FBI arrested Minakuchi and alleged he was distributing pro-Japanese propaganda. He was released after a year in a Maryland internment camp.

After his release, Minakuchi moved to New York and Pennsylvania, where he worked as a butler and became a naturalized citizen. After his wife's death, he returned to Vermont, where he died one year before President Gerald Ford apologized for the internments of Japanese Americans.

Chapter 38

THE JEWISH FAMILY STORE

From 1889 to 1990, there were more than 454 different Jewish-owned retail businesses in downtown Asheville. These merchants were instrumental in creating what we know today as downtown Asheville. Why did these merchants come to Asheville; why were they even merchants?
—Jan Schochet

It is hard to overstate the impact of Jewish merchants on downtown Asheville. Whole blocks of stores on the town's main streets—South and North Main, Patton and Haywood—were owned by Jewish merchants. From the late 1890s and into the 1930s, on South Main alone some of the main merchants were the Lipinsky family's Bon Marche, Morris Meyers's Palais Royal, Strauss European Hotel, Arthur M. Field Co. (jeweler), A. Whitlock Clothing House, Michalove's grocery, Sender Argintar's Uncle Sams Loan Office, Finkelstein's pawnshop, R.B. Zagier's men's clothing shop, Globe Shoes and L. Blomberg's the Racket Store.

What were relations like between the Jewish community and their neighbors? Barred from joining country clubs or buying homes in certain neighborhoods, were Jewish families discriminated against in other ways, and how were these ostracisms felt in daily interactions? What were the relations between the Jewish and black communities? We probed these questions at a 2005 event at the library, Missing History: The Family Store. Asheville native Jan Schochet presided over a panel of four guests: Skip Pearlman, David Schulman, Ellen Carr and Dennis Winner. All of the

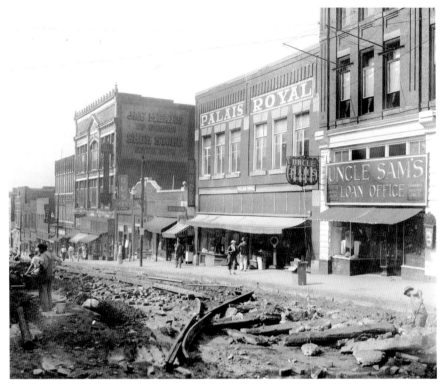

The removal of streetcar tracks from Biltmore Avenue when it was widened in 1934. *K373-4.*

panelists came from families that owned businesses in Asheville, but Carr's Tops for Shoes is the only one still in operation today.

Schochet began with an overview of Jewish merchants in downtown Asheville, reporting that, from the 1880s through the 1980s, there were over 450 such merchants downtown. She explained that Jews in Europe often weren't allowed to own land or enter into trade professions, so many became merchants, a practice they continued after immigrating to the United States. There were businesses such as the Baltimore Bargain House, which would set up an individual with merchandise to peddle until he became prosperous enough to own his own store.

At the end of the program, we asked the panelists to share memorable stories from their family stores, and they delivered the goods.

David Schulman: "As I tend to love the more humorous side of things, here's a little story of stark differences in background. After I married my first wife, who had grown up in New York, Nancy came to work with me one day in Sylva. A preacher I knew well came in our store to kindly introduce himself to my new wife, and upon hearing that she was Jewish, thought she would be pleased to know they had just come back from visiting her 'homeland,' meaning a trip to Israel. Nancy was infuriated and said to him, 'Oh, you just came back from Long Island?'"

Dennis Winner: "I have no stories to add other than with respect to my dad warning Irene Alexander that she would have nasty things said to her. In fact, that did happen for a while." Winner told about his father wanting to hire a black salesperson. His father visited the manager of Bon Marche and several other stores and asked them to do the same on a certain day. Irene Alexander had previously worked as his elevator operator, and he recruited her as a salesperson while warning her that it might be difficult.

Ellen Carr: "One of our first employees at the Bargain Center [where Downtown Books and News is now] was Quanita Leake, who worked for us for thirty-eight years [including work up the street at Tops]. She was African

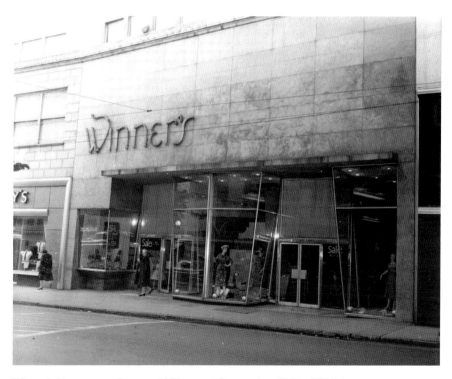

Winner's Department Store at 34 Haywood Street, circa 1950s. *B355-4.*

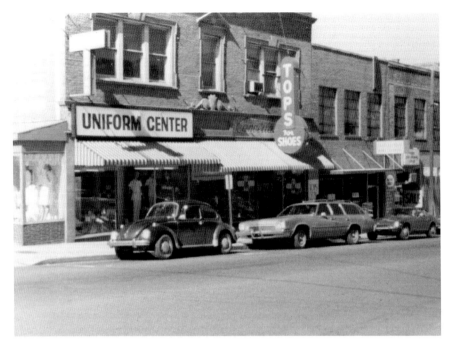

The Uniform Center and Tops for Shoes, located at 23 and 27 Lexington Avenue, were owned and operated by Sylvia and Louis Resnikoff. Photo taken in 1975. *L802-DS.*

American and so shy when she started that she used to hide behind the clothes in the Bargain Center. My mother fired her, and then her mother came and begged for her job back. She turned out to be one of our best employees ever.

"Another incident involved our salesman Jason Gaddy, who's still with us, who felt a woman's toe to see if the shoe fit. She had a very sore toe, and when he touched the toe, she clobbered him on the head so hard she almost knocked him out.

"Our staff always used to dress up at Halloween. One of our employees, Evan Sluder, dressed in head-to-toe black and had chains hanging from his waist and earrings in his ears. A customer came up to him and said, 'I like the way your employees dress up for Halloween.' He said, 'It's great, isn't it? Next year, I'm going to dress up, too.'"

Jan Schochet: "There are a bazillion stories, customers, salesmen, employees that I remember. But something I totally remember: When we took the dance clothing and shoes out of the Star Bootery [16 Patton Avenue] to open A Dancer's Place at 14 Patton in August 1978, I was working with one of our customers who was a dancer. She had graduated from high school and she was my assistant manager, her first full-time job, I think. She lived in Mills River. I don't think it was right at the beginning, but within the first year maybe, a guy breezed in. A large guy about six feet, square shape, nice big-city clothing black pants, white shirt and slicked-back black hair. He breezed in and exclaimed loudly, 'I'm from New York, and I know *all* of these leotards.' (To eliminate shoplifting, I'd designed a way to pin up all our leotards on the walls—it was like an art gallery of dancewear.)

"He'd go up to one shiny red one with little straps and say, 'I've got that one. I wore it to a party last New Year's Eve.' Then, 'I love *that* one'—a sleek black number with velvet straps and rhinestones on the straps—'it's one of my favorite ones!'

"He asked us, 'Am I the first cross-dresser you've had in here?' We looked at each other and said at the same time, 'Probably not, no.' He seemed disappointed. He went on like this for twenty minutes or more, extolling all of our styles. He kept looking back at us as though he were shocking the heck out of us. We just looked at each other and smiled. We were from Asheville, and we'd both already seen a lot, both in the store and in our everyday lives. He was no surprise to us, although we knew he thought he would be. But he was surely one of the most animated, energetic and enthusiastic customers we ever had. I don't even remember if he bought anything. If he did, it was only something like shiny tights."

We also asked, since downtown businesses were closed on Sundays, whether Jewish merchants close on Saturdays, or at least on High Holy Days, and if so, whether that was accepted by the non-Jewish patrons.

Dennis Winner: "No Jewish merchant could be closed on Saturday and survive. Winner's always closed on the High Holy Days."

Jan Schochet: "No store could be closed on Saturday and survive. That is true. There were more shoppers downtown on Saturday than all the other days combined. That is when everyone was off work and when they planned to shop, as they went to church on Sundays and Asheville had blue laws prohibiting stores from being open on Sundays. I don't think any Jewish merchants in Asheville closed on Saturdays. The majority that I knew were Reform, and there were no Reform services on Saturday. We always went to temple on Friday nights.

"But when I was really little, all the downtown stores stayed open late on Friday nights. My parents and uncle did too. At least for part of the year—maybe fall and Christmas season. I assume they figured they'd forgo the religion to get their family on solid footing with the income. Always,

always, always closed for Rosh Hashanah and Yom Kippur. My dad would put a handwritten sign (in his terrible scrawl—he was always teased that he should have been a doctor because of his terrible handwriting) on the door at closing the day before. Just a sheet of paper that said, 'Closed Monday (or whatever day he referred to) for religious observance.' I do know a lot of people would come to the store and be disappointed. But many came back the next time they could and would say, 'We came and you were closed. So we're coming back today.' Not sure if they felt inconvenienced (I don't remember that vibe) or out of admiration (don't remember that vibe either—just a statement of fact)."

Ellen Carr: "We have always been open on Saturday, that being the best day of the week by far. We have never opened on the High Holy Days of Rosh Hashanah or Yom Kippur. This is a tradition that my parents started and we have kept going."

David Schulman: "My parents' business as well as my businesses and the two other Jewish businesses in Sylva were always open on Saturday, as it was until the last couple of decades or so the busiest day of the week. I guess it was a practical compromise all of us felt God would understand. As well as, being open on Sunday would have been looked upon as rude to our gentile customers back then, we thought. I think Sky City Discount was the first retail in the area to open on Sundays, then Kmart, etc."

Skip Pearlman: "During the presence of the business in downtown locations, the business was closed on Sundays and the Jewish holidays of Rosh Hashanah and Yom Kippur. In 1973 or thereabouts, that changed. The business moved to Tunnel Road, diagonally across from the Asheville Mall. Sunday openings had become commonplace as many businesses left downtown Asheville. I personally had a more secular approach to being observant. Bottom line: we stayed open on Sundays and Jewish holidays."

PART VII

GETTING AROUND

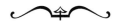

Chapter 39

CONSIDER THE HORSE

The first time I was taken aback by the notion of horses being the main mode of transportation was when I read a short notice in the Daily Citizen *on May 24, 1899, that O.D. Revell's horse took fright while he was inspecting some building work on Spruce Street. The horse made a wild run for College Street and then went on to North Main, the buggy that it was drawing seemingly striking almost every wagon it encountered as it flew by. Now, honestly, when you think of Richard Sharp Smith, Albert Tennent or O.D. Revell going about town, do you picture them on horses? An architect rode a horse-drawn carriage to his clients' homes! Or to inspect one of his buildings under construction! The second time that I envisioned Asheville replete with horses was when I read Pauline Moore's diary.*

To envision a different Asheville, read Pauline Moore's diary, which she wrote in 1916 at the age of nineteen. In May, Pauline wrote, "Frank Netherland & I went for a long horseback ride this afternoon. Up by Beaumont Lodge by the Battle Bungalow through Kenilworth up to the old water works & beyond and home again by the river road & Biltmore."

In Pauline's diary, we see a town not of roads and automobiles and trucks but one traversed with horse trails and paths, with people and their horses everywhere, riding from one place to another across surprising distances.

Later, in August, Pauline wrote, "Icky & I went for a long horseback ride this afternoon out to the Asheville School Lake Dam and came home by a different road. I enjoyed it as much as any ride I have taken this summer." ("Icky" was the nickname for Francis C. Bourne, whom Pauline later married.) Pauline died in Asheville in 1979.

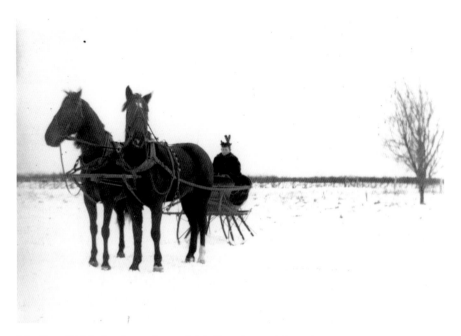

Mrs. Leva Wright in a horse-drawn sleigh. Location and date of the photo are unknown. *G287-4.*

Archived photographs tell us much about what Asheville looked like with horses and all that horses were used for. Horses pulled street-cleaning wagons, laundry wagons and funeral caskets and compelled carriages through very poor roads. They helped the mailwoman deliver mail and took teachers into hard-to-get-to places in the mountains. In fact, they were used for general all-around transportation for most everyone. In short, there were horses just everywhere.

Every sort of tourist brochure about Asheville at the turn of the century listed the best drives and their distances from the center of Asheville—Fernihurst, Richmond Hill, Sunset Drive, the top of Town Mountain, Biltmore and more.

And if you didn't own your own horse or you were visiting, there were at least eight large livery stables in the early 1900s where you could rent one. You could get a horse and buggy for $2.50 or $3.00 a day or a two-horse surrey for the same price. You could even rent your own tallyho for $8.00 to $10.00; it was drawn by four horses and could hold ten to fourteen passengers.

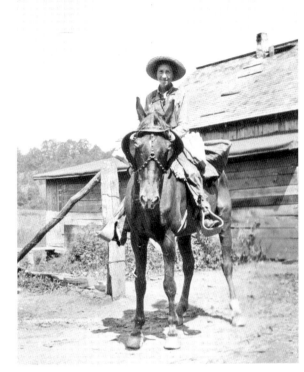

Right: Sandy Mush mail carrier Ethel Surrett riding horseback to deliver mail to rural customers. *MS247.002L photo K.*

Below: A woman in a horse-drawn carriage surveys Biltmore Village. All Souls Church is on her left, while the original Kenilworth Inn, built in 1890, looms above. Photo taken in 1903. *A286-5.*

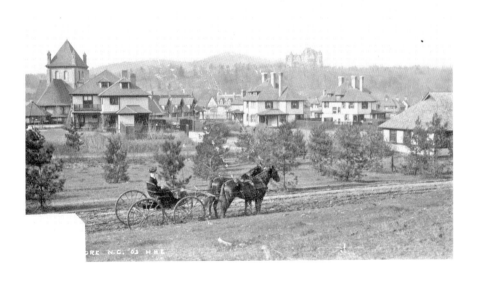

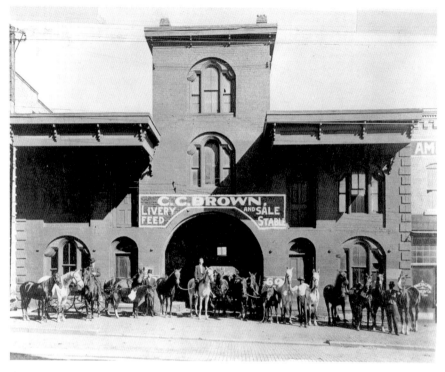

C.C. Brown Livery Barn, located at 56–60 South Main Street, in 1912. Earlier, the building had served as an opera house and a tobacco warehouse. *B633-8.*

And when the first automobile came through Asheville in March 1900, we all know what it was called—a horseless carriage. "It doesn't shy at trolley cars, and it stands anywhere without hitching," the *Asheville Daily Citizen* noted in a March 12 article headlined "Horseless Carriage Makes Its Appearance."

Even today, travel by horse isn't strictly a thing of the past. Twice now, the staff at Pack Memorial Library has happened to see women traveling alone on horseback cross-country, riding through Asheville on their way. The first one stopped by the library and hitched her horse outside the Children's Room.

It reminded us: do you know there are still some rings around town, buried in old curbs, where people used to tie up their horses?

Chapter 40

ASHEVILLE'S FIRST MOTOR MILE:
COXE AVENUE

Asheville's first Motor Mile was downtown's Coxe Avenue. While a new auto district has emerged in recent years along Brevard Road in West Asheville, in the 1950s and '60s—the peak years of the American automobile industry and the years remembered for the hype of the annual model change—Coxe was the place for checking out the latest automotive wares.

I t is hard to describe the excitement that the annual introduction of the new cars produced. The model changeover was always timed for the early fall. The so-called Big Three—General Motors, Ford and Chrysler—invested millions of dollars in making each year's model appear substantially different from the year before. Often, this was just a change of sheet metal, but every few years, the entire platform of a car would be changed. The best-remembered change of the era was the introduction of the 1955 Chevrolet, described as "The Hot One"—and hot it was, especially when compared with the now stodgy-appearing models of 1954.

Let's pretend it's the fall of 1957 and we're taking a stroll down Coxe Avenue. One of the master automotive stylists of the era, Dick Teague, called this the "age of gorp." Chrome trim and tail fins were being applied in vast quantities to automobiles and then rearranged the following year to create the impression that there was something new underneath the pizzazz. Heading south from the Patton Avenue intersection and past the Trailways bus terminal on the right and the Sears department store on the left, we enter automobile row and something resembling a small-town

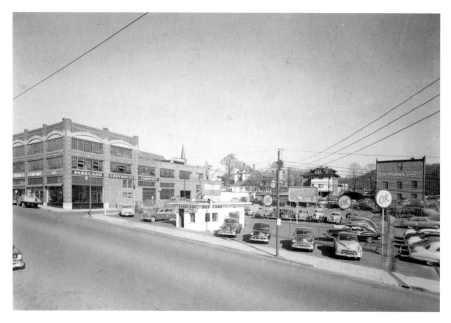

Coxe Avenue facing north toward Parkland Chevrolet, circa 1954. *B395-8.*

carnival. Banners and pennants are flying, and the sidewalks are crowded, especially if it's a Friday evening or a Saturday.

The big automotive news of 1958 was Ford's introduction of the Edsel. Asheville's Edsel dealership was Sam's, on North Market Street. The reaction to the new marque was immediate and harsh. The father of former Pack Memorial Library director Ed Sheary, who never missed the new model introduction despite the fact that he usually kept a car for close to a decade, described the Edsel as much too ugly to sell. He was proven right about that; the model was dead and gone in three years. He also found little to like in the new Chevrolets at the Parkland dealership at 50 Coxe Avenue. "Tortured sheet metal," he called them.

The new Fords, from Matthews Motors, then still at 100 Coxe Avenue before the company's move to Biltmore Avenue in 1960, were more to his liking. Not that he bought one; there would be no new Ford in the Sheary driveway until 1963. The Plymouth-Dodge and Oldsmobile dealers were around the corner at 226 and 196 Hilliard Avenue. The lower end of Coxe Avenue was home to used car lots and a variety of automobile repair shops. The best known of the used car dealers was Bob Ledford's at 185 Coxe Avenue.

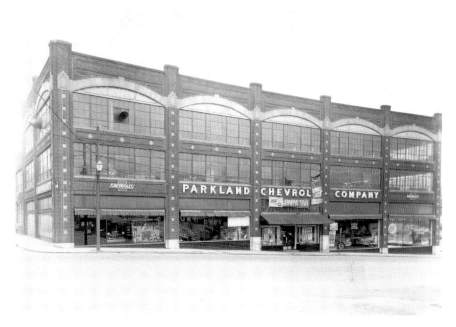

Parkland Chevrolet at 54 Coxe Avenue, in the former Richbourg Motor Company building, 1953–54. *B351-8.*

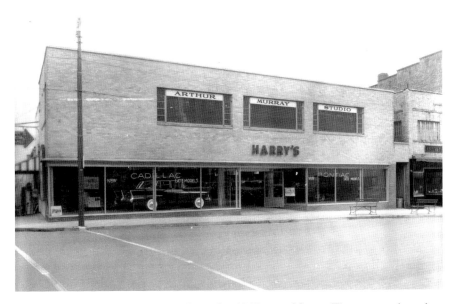

Harry's Cadillac-Pontiac showroom, located at 69 Haywood Street. The car seen through the window appears to be a 1957 Vauxhall imported by Pontiac. The second floor housed the Arthur Murray dance studio. *B338-4.*

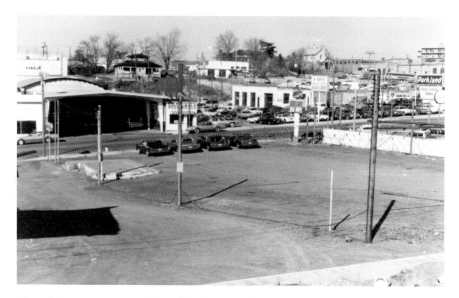

View of Coxe Avenue, east side parking lot, across from Harry's Used Cars, 1979. Parkland Auto Center Sales is also visible. *MS184.003C.*

There were a few outliers from Coxe Avenue among the new car dealers, including Glover Chrysler-Plymouth at the corner of Valley and College Streets and Ed Orr Motors at 90 Biltmore Avenue, which sold Ramblers out of the building that currently houses the French Broad Food Co-op. Sam's Lincoln Mercury was on North Market Street, and the best-known dealership of them all, Harry's Cadillac-Pontiac, was on Haywood Street, the current site of Pack Memorial Library.

Coxe and nearby Hilliard Avenue was the center of the automotive action, and all of the dealerships were within easy walking distance to downtown. By the mid-1960s, though, times were definitely changing. The Ford dealership was by then well established on Biltmore Avenue, and Dorato Dodge could be found on Tunnel Road. The permanent end of the dominance of Coxe Avenue and downtown Asheville as the region's automotive marketplace was marked by the move of Harry's to the West Asheville end of Patton Avenue in the 1970s. J.L. Cannon Motors opened on Tunnel Road, selling Volkswagens in the building that is now the site of Prestige Subaru.

It had been great fun while it lasted, but the annual model change was soon to be presaged by the arrival of Ralph Nader, pollution controls and a tidal wave of imported cars that all looked the same to the denizens of Asheville's original Motor Mile.

Chapter 41

ASHEVILLE'S LANDING STRIPS

Convenient air travel from Asheville continues to expand. For example, you can now fly to locations in Florida from Asheville on a budget airline in under two hours, with no stops. Lovely—but it makes us wonder how it used to be.

Asheville's first landing strip was on what was known as Baird's Bottom, the land that was later flooded to create Beaver Lake, which is owned and maintained by the North Asheville residents of Lake View Park.

In the photo on the following page, taken on June 19, 1919, Henry Westall prepares to take off from Baird's Bottom in his plane, the *Asheville*. Westall was a U.S. Army Signal Corps pilot in World War I and started a commercial aviation business here in 1919, with shares selling for fifty dollars each. He purchased a surplus Canadian training plane and some aircraft parts, and voila, the Asheville Aerial Corporation was in business. Rides over Asheville were available for fifteen dollars, a hefty sum at the time. Also in 1919, Westall was the first aviator to fly over the Blue Ridge Mountains. It took him less than an hour to fly from Asheville to Morganton. The rest of the story is hearsay but interesting: Westall flew for only about eighteen months, and on his last flight, after landing, he kissed the wing of his plane and never flew again.

The second landing strip was Dillingham Field, established in 1920 when Scott Dillingham turned a cornfield in Haw Creek into an airfield. Dillingham bought Westall's plane, hired a pilot and also went into the

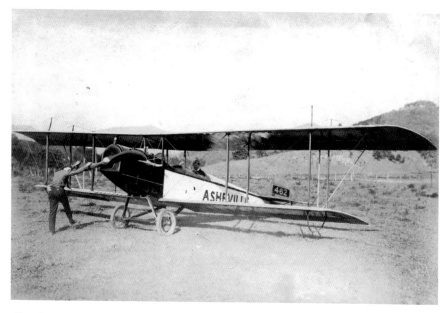

Above: Henry Westall on June 19, 1919, preparing to take off from Baird's Bottom (now the bed of Beaver Lake) in his plane the *Asheville*. *A009-8.*

Opposite, top: Mrs. Vance Spivey sports aviator's clothing at the Emma Air Park, a fourteen-acre tract located a half mile west of Emma, 1948. *N863-5b.*

Opposite, bottom: Airplanes in front of the hangar at the Emma Air Park, 1948. *N863-5a.*

passenger flying business. His organization flew sightseers over Asheville for two dollars (a substantial reduction from Westall's fifteen dollars).

Our next "airport" was Emma Air Park, a fourteen-acre tract located about a half mile west of Emma. In the top photo on the facing page, Mrs. Vance Spivey (in aviator's clothing) looks to board one of the small planes to her left.

On January 24, 1928, Harry Brooks, Henry Ford's test pilot, attempted to fly from Ford Field in Dearborn, Michigan, to Miami, Florida. This first long-distance attempt in the *Ford Flivver* landed short in a forced landing at Emma Air Park. However, Brooks did set a nonstop distance record in his small single-seat, thirty-six-horsepower plane. The Detroit craft flew 790 miles on twenty gallons of gas. Brooks was killed in a crash in 1929, and his death, along with the economic depression, caused Ford to pull out of the business of manufacturing airplanes.

Owen Field in West Asheville was our next airport. It was originally called Carrier Field, from the days when it was used for horse racing. It was

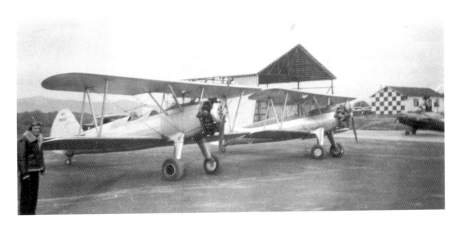

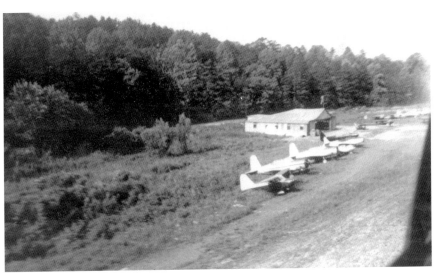

renamed for Dr. James E. Owen, a local dentist and old-time barnstorming aviator. After the airport closed, the Asheville Speedway was built on the site, opening as a dirt track in 1961 and paved for the 1962 season. The Speedway closed after the 1999 season, and the land was converted to a city recreational place that we enjoy today as Carrier Park.

As early as 1925, the Asheville Chamber of Commerce recognized the possibilities for tourism and appointed a committee to research areas for a future airport. In 1936, Asheville and Hendersonville together purchased the land for an airport, which was operated from 1943 to 1947 by the U.S. Army Corps of Engineers. During this time, the federal Works Progress Administration spent $170,000 to build runways. Known as the Asheville-

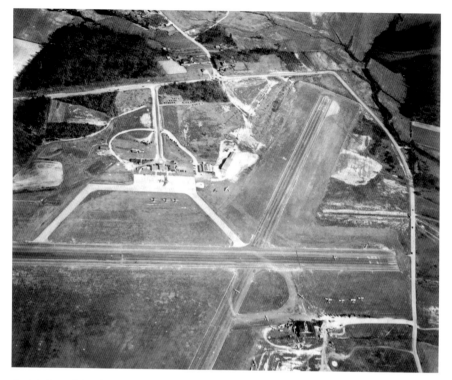

Aerial view of the Asheville-Hendersonville Airport, March 1950. *H102-4.*

Hendersonville Airport or sometimes Lakeside Airport, it was located in the Arden-Fletcher area, where larger tracts of flat land were available. Delta, Capital and Piedmont Airlines all flew into this airfield.

By the late 1950s, air travel was increasingly popular, and there was a need for a larger airport with longer runway capacity to handle bigger, speedier aircraft. Another tract of land was purchased—this one about three miles to the west of the earlier Asheville-Hendersonville Airport. In January 1961, just a few months behind schedule, the new Asheville Regional Airport opened. Today, the airport continues to grow with its traditional carriers—Delta, United and US Airways (now American)—and by adding new carriers like Allegiant. In recent years, the facility has posted successive records for traffic, serving more than 950,000 passengers in 2017.

Chapter 42

THREE MOUNTAIN TOLL ROADS

In November 1912, *Motor Age* magazine heralded the delights of "an exclusive road for motor cars" with "nearly all of it at a 3 to 5 percent grade." E.W. Grove of St. Louis and Asheville was responsible for creating the road up to and beyond the Grove Park Inn. The entire length of the road, from near the end of Charlotte Street to the summit of Sunset Mountain, was "laid with macadam and rolled until its surface is as smooth as a floor." It was wide enough for "speeding motors to pass at any point," and there were signs at approaches to curves for motorists to blow their horns. At the crest, the road connected to a proposed but unfinished Blue Ridge Highway from Asheville to Blowing Rock. At that time, only fifty miles from the Blowing Rock end were completed; from the Asheville end, there was only a horseback trail to Mount Mitchell. The toll was fifty cents for one-seat cars and seventy-five cents for two-seaters.

The text of a *Visit Sunset Mountain* sales brochure extolled the wonders to be seen from the road. The pamphlet dates after 1931 because it mentions Blue Briar Cottage, where "Herbert Hoover, Jr. regained his health" during a visit that year. Also, it stated that "there was a level space for parking and a shop for the sale of rugs, pottery, and native crafts at the summit."

The back page of the pamphlet announced that the present owners of Sunset Mountain lived in Monaco and that it was for sale as a whole or in part by the Sunset Estate Company. In 1950, the collection of tolls on the road ceased.

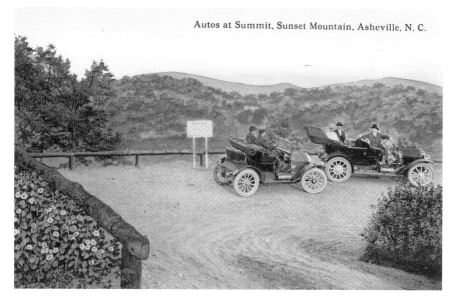

Autos at Summit, Sunset Mountain, Asheville, N. C.

*A postcard view of early automobiles at the summit of Sunset Mountain, circa 1907–15.
AA472.*

Two other toll roads existed in Buncombe County in the early twentieth century. In the west, Highway 151 winding up to Mount Pisgah from the head of Hominy Valley was once a private, one-lane carriage road built by George Vanderbilt to access his Buck Springs Lodge sometime between 1915 and 1917. Later, it opened as a toll road, with one way up the mountain in the mornings and one way down in the afternoon. The toll was seventy-five cents. No one knows precisely where the tollhouse was originally located, but it's thought it was in the area that is now a campground, just as Highway 151 makes a sharp left turn to ascend the mountain. The tollhouse cottage was given to Chester and Ruby Cogburn before or shortly after they opened for business as Pisgah View Ranch in 1941. The cottage—one of the guest cabins—still stands at Pisgah View Ranch.

At the eastern end of Buncombe County, the Mount Mitchell Railroad was built in 1912 to carry timber and lumber down the mountains. Because of tourism's benefits, a passenger train to Camp Alice was quickly added to transport visitors. By 1921, the lumber supply was exhausted. The railroad tracks were pulled up and the rail bed converted into a single-lane toll road. Opening in June 1922, tolls were one dollar per adult and fifty cents for children between the ages of five and twelve.

196:—On the Mt. Mitchell Motor Road, Western North Carolina.

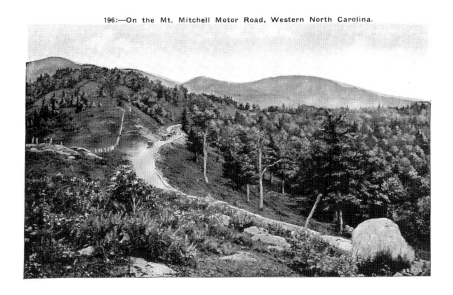

1920s automobiles travel along a dirt road on their climb up Mount Mitchell. *AB574.*

Like the toll road to Mount Pisgah, there were scheduled times for going up and coming back down the road. The road closed in 1939 when the Blue Ridge Parkway opened.

PART VIII

QUIRKS AND KERFUFFLES

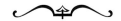

Chapter 43

THE MIKADO ROOM—AN ASHEVILLE ORIGINAL

The train reached Asheville in 1880 for the first time, and things would never be the same. The town became a true destination, ushering in unexpected changes and new kinds of culture.

On what may have been a crisp January evening in 1886, four young men returned from seeing the *Mikado* at the Asheville Opera House on Patton Avenue. With music and lyrics by Gilbert and Sullivan, the production had opened in London in March 1885. It was an immediate success, and by the end of 1885, some 150 companies in Europe and America were producing the opera. Remarkably, less than a year after its London debut, it arrived in the mountains of Western North Carolina.

The *Mikado*, and all things Japanese, became a craze. Although we sometimes think of the 1920s as the height of American interest in Japan—with women wearing kimonos and playing mahjongg—it was actually a much earlier fad. In the late nineteenth century, Americans and Europeans were captivated by Japanese arts and customs. Aestheticism, which leaned heavily on the Orient for design motifs, was all the rage in furniture and home wares. And once the Arts and Crafts movement took hold in the early twentieth century, many artists became enamored with Japanese woodblock print.

Our four young men, J. Taylor Amiss, Fred Jacobs, Edwin Gatchell and Roger Davis, were fascinated by the *Mikado*, and on their return to the flat of

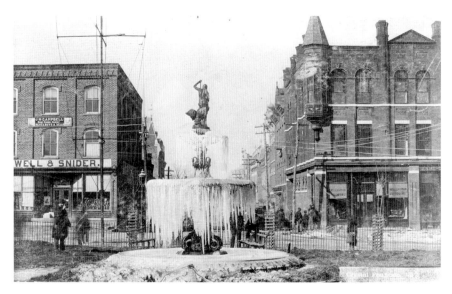

A winter scene: a frozen fountain in Court Square (later Pack Square), looking down Patton Avenue. *Originally published by Lindsey & Brown in the book* Land of the Sky, *1890.*

Amiss and Jacobs, which was located above Lyon's drugstore, they discussed the production.

At some point in the evening's conversation, one of the men suggested turning the flat into a Mikado room. In an article published in *Dixie*, an illustrated magazine from Atlanta, is this quote: "Boys, why don't you make of this a Mikado room? They all heartily fell in with the idea saying: Just the thing, by Jove! By all means have a Mikado room."

With alacrity and creativity, the young men, led by Davis (who was the artist of the group and nicknamed Crayon), began their project. When asked if it was necessary that everything in the room be of Japanese design, Crayon replied, "By no means, it is mainly in the decorations that we must adhere as closely as may be to the Orient. We shall leave the furniture… but everything we add should be as characteristic of Japan as possible." He continued, "I would suggest you have the floor painted in imitation walnut and oak marquetry, have the ceiling tinted and the walls papered. I would have a paper of neutral tint, and the ceiling a light blue."

Not having much money, they gathered material they felt gave the sense of the Far East from local sources, adding paper lanterns and parasols, brackets, scarves, easels, picture frames and fringing. The Mikado room became a reality and the darling of Asheville and beyond. Once it was completed, the

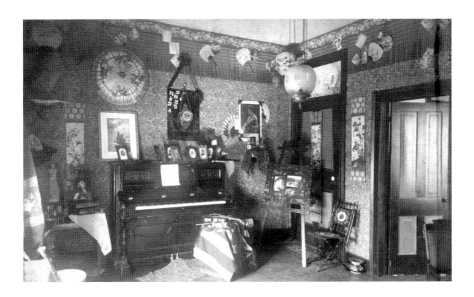

Above: The finished Mikado room with piano at the ready. *MS291.001.*

Right: Another view of the Mikado room—probably Roger Davis, aka Crayon, at the easel. *MS291.020.*

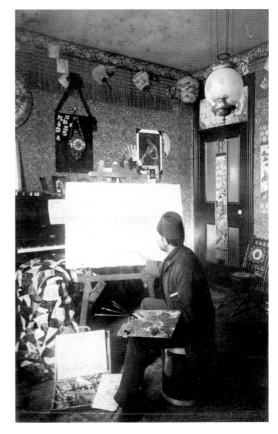

young men gave recitals and dinner parties and enjoyed showing their space to visitors. Several local and distant newspapers picked up the story of the space, calling it "The Southern Mikado Room."

Eventually, the young men moved on with their lives, and the Mikado room became a distant memory. J. Taylor Amiss married in the summer of 1886, and we can thank his wife, who put together a scrapbook on the room. The North Carolina Room now has rare documentation on this small and charming piece of Asheville history.

Chapter 44

THERE'S NOTHING LIKE A PICNIC

The word picnic *derives from a seventeenth-century French word of unknown origin,* picque-nique, *but according to the* Oxford English Dictionary, *second edition, the term* picnic *did not appear in the English language until around 1800. It describes the meaning as similar to today's: "A fashionably social entertainment in which each person present contributed a share of the provisions." Picque-nique, which became our word* picnic, *is "each pick a bit."*

There *is* nothing like a picnic. Hardboiled eggs are a favorite, as are pies. Some folks prefer a blanket on the ground. Most important is a pretty spot outdoors, such as the one chosen by the J.D. Earle family.

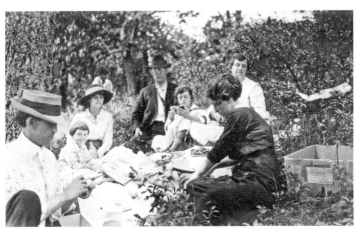

The Earle family picnic includes J.D. Earle, *at left in hat,* and Bess Earle, *thought to be the woman on the right.* The card stock on which this photo is printed dates it to 1904–18. *MS222.001I.*

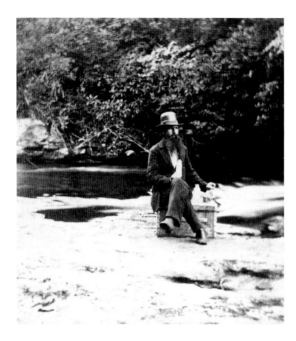

Left: Man perched on his picnic basket beside a river. *G267-5.*

Opposite, top: A group of diners seated at an outdoor table. *From right*, they are Ruby Creasman, photographer George Masa, mother Effie Creasman, father Oscar Creasman, Doris Creasman, Blanche Creasman, cousin Lelia Pressley, Blake Creasman and an unidentified man. *MA100-4.*

Opposite, bottom: Photographer Herbert Pelton's family and friends enjoy a picnic on the rocks. Wife Allie Vivian Moore Pelton is at far left; the dark-haired man may be Pelton, circa 1920s. *L503-4.*

This man chose to sit on his picnic basket while eating a baguette beside the river.

The Oscar Creasman family chose an outdoor table with a pretty tablecloth strewn across it. Foods are, unfortunately, not identifiable. Note the second person from right is George Masa, well-known Asheville photographer. The photograph on the top of the facing page is from a collection donated by Jeanne Creasman Lance in 2000. Jeanne Lance said that George Masa lived with her family for several years, she thinks between 1915 and 1920.

Some people have their favorite picnic basket, some of which may have been passed down through the family. Old wicker baskets are pieces of art in themselves. In the photo on the bottom of the facing page, note the small feast spread out by the well-known Asheville photographer Herbert W. Pelton with family beside a mountain stream. His second wife, Allie Vivian Moore Pelton, is on the far left.

The historic place to picnic in Asheville was on top of Beaucatcher Mountain. In *Look Homeward, Angel*, Thomas Wolfe wrote a beautiful passage about Eugene taking Laura on an outing there. The young couple took a shoebox to a little grocery on Woodfin Street and bought "crackers, peanut butter, currant jelly, bottled pickles, and a big slice of rich yellow cheese." On the way, they stopped off at Eugene's sister's house (assumed to refer to Wolfe's sister Mabel), and in the lusty way typical of the Wolfe family, she

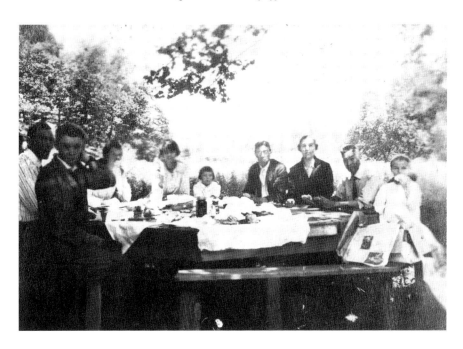

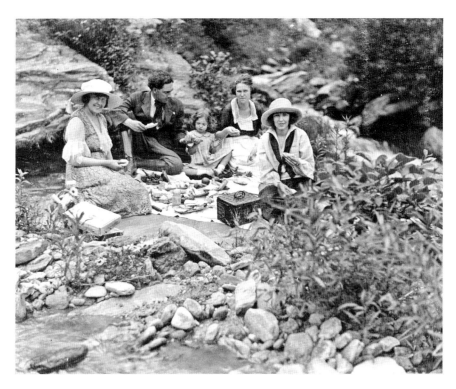

continued to add to their box boiled eggs and sandwiches. As they were leaving, she met them on the front porch with another shoebox "stuffed with sandwiches, boiled eggs and fudge."

"They climbed sharply up, along a rock trail, avoiding the last long corkscrew of the road, and stood in the gap, at the road's summit," the story continues. "They were only a few hundred feet above the town: it lay before them with the sharp nearness of a Sienese picture, at once close and far....But the hills were lordly, with a plan. Westward they widened into the sun, soaring up from buttressing shoulders. The town was thrown up on the plateau like an encampment: there was nothing below him that could resist time."

Chapter 45

ASHEVILLE'S BLUE LAWS

The history of Asheville's Sunday blue laws is a little hard to pin down, and they changed over time. In general, legislation banning the sale of booze on Sunday emphasized the idea of "rest for toilers and the assurance of avoiding giving offense by noise and tumult," a city ordinance noted in 1884. Many cities and states had them, and some still do. In most of North Carolina, it is still illegal to sell alcohol on Sundays before noon, though the so-called brunch bill has been used in recent years to lower the hour for sales in municipalities across the state, including Asheville.

It appears, through local records and newspaper coverage of blue laws, that they were mostly meant to keep Sundays un-commercialized, in keeping with the idea of having a day of rest. In *Charter and Ordinances of the City of Asheville, June 1884*, it says that no person should be allowed to load or unload any wagon used for hauling on the Sabbath; sell or give away any intoxicating drinks; or keep a barbershop open on Sunday.

Over time, amendments and additional ordinances augmented and altered the blue laws:

- In 1898, the aldermen voted unanimously to allow the sale of ice on Sunday.
- In 1899, the police visited the Candy Kitchen, then at 28 Patton Avenue, to uphold a blue law, asserting that "one could not order ice cream on Sunday without first taking a lunch and that lunch could not consist of cake." The proprietor, Mr.

Theobold, solved that situation by sending out for a ham so that sandwiches could be served before the ice cream dessert.

- In 1905, the aldermen adopted a "liberal" ordinance to allow the selling of soda water, fruits and candies on Sunday. The following day, a meeting of indignant Asheville ministers was held to protest the measure.
- Jumping ahead to April 1934, the entertainment ban was lifted by city council. It allowed for Sunday amusements, declaring that baseball and theaters were okay between the hours of 1:00 and 7:00 p.m. (On May 6, 1934, over six thousand people attended McCormick Field and theaters for the first Sunday in Asheville's history.) Billiards and bowling were still forbidden at any time on Sunday, and the new ordinance also retained a ban on conducting most kinds of business on Sunday. This did not apply to filling stations, garages, drugstores and bakeries, which could be open for business for certain items.

A number of discount and chain stores began moving into town, and they were in the habit of being open on Sundays in other places. But Asheville voters pushed back and, in 1965, voted 7,378 to 6,552 to approve a harsh new blue law. City manager J. Weldon Wier summarized its wide sweep: "If you can't eat it, read it or use it on your person, it is illegal to sell it." Items such as furniture, clothing and hardware could not be sold. While working on how to enforce the restrictions, Police Chief A.R. Sluder commented, "A man can buy a house on Sunday but he can't buy something to put on his back if he is cold."

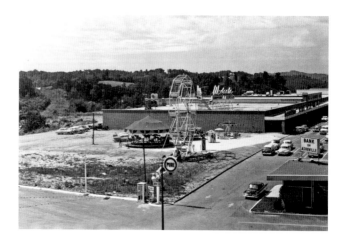

Elevated view of the Westgate Shopping Center in West Asheville. The Bank of Asheville is visible in the right foreground and a Ferris wheel in the center, circa 1958. *B357-4.*

While the ordinance didn't specify which types of merchants must close on Sundays, many stores, including Ingles groceries and K-Mart, recognized the state of public opinion and opted to close.

In 1970, Asheville's blue laws met their demise, with city council voting 4–2 to repeal them once and for all.

Chapter 46

A VERY BIG BOY

North Carolina Room staff value the times they are able to work together with their sister county agencies, especially with the registrar and staff of the Buncombe County Register of Deeds. Drew Reisinger's work made Buncombe County the first county in the state of North Carolina to put its slave deeds online, and he is currently working with other counties in the state to do the same. After we posted "A Very Big Boy," Drew wrote to us that one of his staff had actually found a bill of sale for Big Boy. It completed our story, giving us the information of the two men who owned him and what happened to him afterward.

In mid-June 1939, a yellow-trimmed, red trailer home equipped with air conditioning, two sound systems and electric lights rolled into downtown Asheville. Emblazoned on the sides of the trailer were the words "Big Boy."

An advertisement appeared in the *Asheville Citizen* on June 18, 1939: "Everybody see BIG BOY The World's Largest HOG Absolutely Weighs ONE TON, ALIVE! Alive! 4 feet. Patton Avenue at the Bus Station."

Big Boy was born in Black Mountain in 1934 as the only male in a litter of five. His father—a Poland China—had come from Indiana to start a family. His parents weighed in at a measly four or five hundred pounds apiece. Big Boy spent his boyhood days in Black Mountain. By 1938, he tipped the scales of a Black Mountain veterinarian at 1,975 pounds and set out on a tour of North Carolina in the red trailer. According to a delightful article in the January 7, 1939 edition of the *Rocky Mount Telegram*, Big Boy had no address, "for he's a traveling man." The author allowed that Big Boy's visit

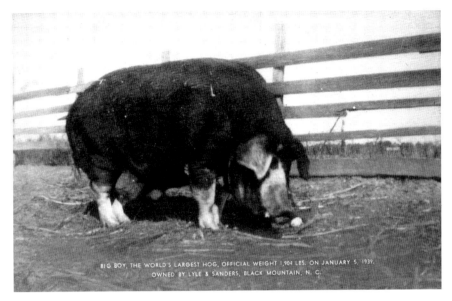

BIG BOY, THE WORLD'S LARGEST HOG, OFFICIAL WEIGHT 1,904 LBS. ON JANUARY 5, 1939.
OWNED BY LYLE & SANDERS, BLACK MOUNTAIN, N. C.

Asheville Postcard Company published "Big Boy, the World's Largest Hog, Official Weight 1,904 lbs. on January 5, 1939. Owned by Lyle & Sanders, Black Mountain, N.C." *AE194.*

in Rocky Mount was a chance to see "potential barbecue on the hoof for 10 cents a view."

Big Boy lost weight on his 1938 statewide tour, despite being fed a daily three gallons of hog ration, corn and "bits of green food." "No slops for this aristocrat," wrote the author of the article in the *Rocky Mount Telegram.* He also received a daily beauty regimen of brushing, spraying and greasing. During the tour, Big Boy had been "handled by strategy and corn": one day, his handler spent three hours coaxing "his hog highness" into the red trailer.

In April 1939, Big Boy made a stop in his birthplace of Black Mountain. The following headline appeared in the *Asheville Citizen-Times* on April 30: "'Big Boy' Giant Hog Displays Temperament as Newsreel Is Made." "Displaying a temperament as erratic and explosive as that of the most eccentric star of stage or screen, 'Big Boy' said to be the world's largest hog, exhibited his nearly a ton of hams, bacon and side meat near Black Mountain yesterday for a Fox Movietone newsreel cameraman and the glory of pigdom and Western North Carolina."

According to the story, Big Boy led a "merry chase about the pasture while a bevy of Black Mountain school girls in shorts," a cameraman, the publicity director for the Asheville Chamber of Commerce and W.H.

Hunnicutt (a Black Mountain attorney) waited for him to calm down. The author of the article wrote that Big Boy had been "cooped up in his show pen for months" and was "squealing with delight and snorting like the exhaust of a ten-ton truck."

When Big Boy calmed down, he allowed the girls to "curry his hair, put a crimp in his tail with a curling iron, and place a ribbon about his neck. Big Boy only objected when his nose was powdered with a huge powder puff."

Plans were in the offing to drive Big Boy up to New York City for the opening of the 1939 New York World's Fair.

The Buncombe County Register of Deeds actually has a bill of sale recorded March 28, 1940. P. Lilies was selling his "one-half interest to One Poland China Hog commonly known as 'big Boy' and weighing 1900 pounds, and being commonly known and advertised as the largest hog in the world and for exhibition purposes." The bill of sale reads, "And being the same hog heretofore owned in the partnership of P. Liles and Herman Sanders." Now we know who the owners were who were mentioned on the postcard. Lilies also sold his one-half interest in "one Chevrolet Truck, 1934 Model, the same being now used as a conveyance in exhibiting the above described hog." The new owner was A.J. Hemphill of Buncombe County.

You just can't make this stuff up. I'm on the hunt for Big Boy's Fox MovieTone newsreel, one of three made in the Asheville area in 1939. Perhaps in the future we'll all be able to see Big Boy gamboling in the field!

PART IX

Asheville Architecture

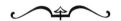

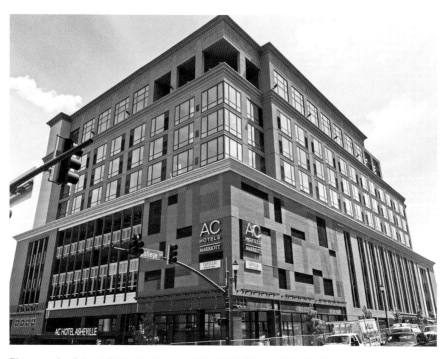

Photograph of the AC Motel taken late July 2017. *Photo by Terry Taylor.*

Chapter 47

STANDING ON ONE CORNER IN ASHEVILLE

S tanding on one corner of Asheville is an excellent place to learn about the ever-changing face of our city. Do you recognize this corner, and are you familiar with its curious history?

James McConnell Smith was born in 1787. According to historical accounts, he was the first white child born west of the Blue Ridge. As a young man (circa 1812), he clerked at the Eagle Hotel, which was first located on Eagle Street and owned by Colonel John Patton. Smith married Polly Patton (the daughter of his employer) in June 1814.

According to a January 1875 account in the *Asheville Weekly Citizen*, Smith made some money doing survey work in 1815, bought some building lots from a butcher named Corn and "ceiled his log cabin, with plank, and to this kept the building for thirty years." This was home for Smith and his wife, on the corner of what was then North Main and College Streets. It once stood on what was then the outer edge of downtown—a hot spot that drovers traveling from Tennessee would first reach as they moved cattle, hogs and other goods to South Carolina.

Smith opened the doors of his home to create the Buck Hotel. As was common in those days, proprietors lived in the building they worked in until they could afford a separate home. In newspapers from 1844 through 1856, the hotel was advertised as J.M. Smith's Hotel but also referred to as the Buck Hotel.

The building was added to over the years to accommodate the demand for rooms in a growing town. You can see in the only known surviving

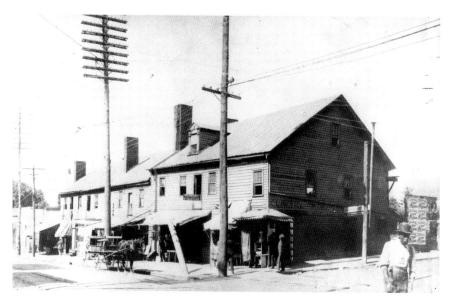

One of Asheville's first hotels, the Buck Hotel stood on Main Street N, now the corner of Broadway and College Street. Built in 1825, it was owned and operated by James McConnell Smith. It became Mrs. Evans's boardinghouse in the 1890s, near the time of this photo, and was demolished in 1907. *A725-8.*

photograph how the hotel was enlarged toward the north in two additions, each requiring a new chimney. The original south end is on the right. In addition to visitors, the Buck was used by a variety of entrepreneurs as their temporary offices.

In addition to his duties as innkeeper, Smith ran a store on the opposite side of North Main, maintained a "tanyard" on the south side of town and purchased and managed the first bridge across the French Broad River, which was known as Smith's Bridge. He was a landowner in Buncombe County as well as Georgia, according to Sondley's *A History of Buncombe County, North Carolina.*

Smith's wife, Polly, the mother of nine surviving children, died in 1853. When Smith died in 1856, he was considered a wealthy man and entailed his various properties to his numerous heirs. His son-in-law J.H. Gudger (married to his eldest daughter, Elizabeth) likely leased the hotel and ran it for several years. During the war years, the hotel also served as the Confederacy's official post office. It was then leased to different managers, who operated it under different names—the Rail Road Hotel, Trout Hotel and Central House, to name a few.

As the years passed, hotels such as the Battery Park and Swannanoa, with their modern amenities, lured fashionable travelers. By the late 1800s, the corner of North Main and College was not the first choice for visitors coming to Asheville. Traveling salesmen did use the premises, along with other sorts of assorted characters.

An eight-story, skeletal form of poured concrete reinforced with steel stood on the corner of North Main and College Streets for about seven years as infighting among the Smith estate's heirs halted construction. An original drawing of the hotel is dated January 1906. This was quite an embarrassment to the architectural firm of Smith & Carrier. Once the estate was settled, two prominent businessmen—John H. Lange and Gay Green—purchased the site to finish the building.

John H. Lange (1868–1924) was raised in the Avery Creek area. He moved to and worked in Spartanburg, South Carolina, before coming to Asheville in the late 1890s. Lange first appeared in the city directory as the manager of the Glen Rock Hotel in 1896–97, as well as the proprietor of a saloon at 15–17 West College Street in 1899–1900. In 1909, Lange organized the Western Carolina Auto Company and was prominent in real estate and development activities in town.

Gay Green (1870–1951) was once described as an "Asheville Capitalist." He was born in the Newfound section of Leicester. Around 1890, Green established a grocery store at the corner of Roberts and Buxton Streets. He sold the store and moved to Watsonville, California, to enter the hotel business. He returned to Asheville in 1902 and founded a furniture business with his brother on Patton Avenue. In 1905, he founded the Imperial Life Insurance Company. He was a prolific buyer of land and properties.

In November 1910, Lange and Green purchased the uncompleted building—then called the Miller Hotel—standing on the corner of North Main and College Streets. The combination of the new owners' surnames formed the name for the soon-to-be-completed building: the Langren Hotel.

Concrete blocks with sixty different patterns were made on the third floor of the hotel. A blacksmith shop was also set up there, and all the iron braces to be used in the roof were made there, according to the *Asheville Citizen* of May 20, 1911. In May 1912, the following headline appeared in the *Asheville Citizen*: "Concrete Hotel Is Rapidly Taking Form." Prominent businessmen, including the photographer H. Taylor Rogers, wrote effusive praise for the new hotel that would open soon in Asheville.

The Langren opened its doors for business on July 4, 1912. The Social Happenings column in the *Asheville Citizen* that day described the banquet

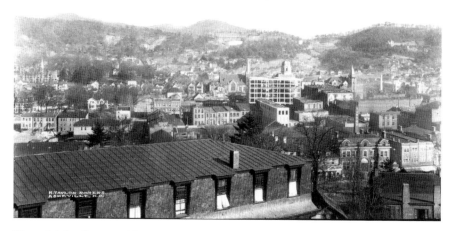

View of Asheville toward Beaucatcher Mountain from the Battery Park Hotel (1886); the top east side of the Hotel appears in the lower left. The shell of the Langren Hotel, completed in 1912, is at right center. The courthouse (1903) dome is visible above the Langren with city hall (1892) beside it. First Baptist Church is just left of the Langren. Asheville Female College is at top left. The Colonial boardinghouse below it is at #58 Broadway. Haywood Street is at lower right, including the Club Café and Candy Kitchen (#21–23), Cruise Hair Dressing Parlor (#25), YMCA (#27) and the Halthenon Building (#29–31). The Mountain City Steam Laundry smokestack stands over the YMCA building on Haywood Street. The sign for Millard Livery, #33–35 Broadway, appears on the rear of the building facing Broadway at the Walnut Street intersection. To its right is the Brown Hardware Company (#25 Broadway). The building to its left with scaffolding against the wall is Cherokee Marble Works (#53 Broadway). The reservoir on Beaucatcher Mountain is at center top. *A223-5.*

and ball to be held in the evening. Prominent local names such as Rankin, Lipinsky, Coxe, Westall, Moore, Wells, Westall, Barnard, Reynolds, McBrayer, Ray and Haynes were just a few of the attendees. The music and dance programs were described in culinary terms: Red Pepper Rag, Chicken Reel, Clam Chowder Rag, Absinthe Frappe and Rock and Rye Two Step. All followed, of course, by cigars and cigarettes. Tickets for the ball could be purchased up until the starting hour of 8:30 p.m. And because many gentlemen were "engaged in business…the occasion will not necessarily be full dress."

The eight-story hotel possessed all modern amenities, including a rooftop garden, a drugstore and a sanitary soda fountain.

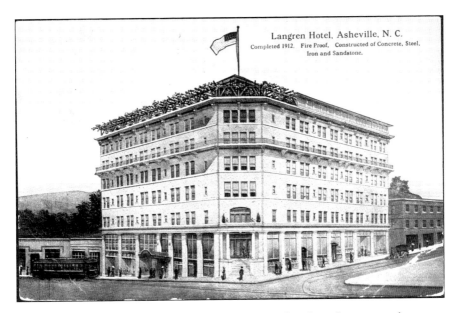

The Langren Hotel opened in 1912 and was located at 8 Broadway. Streetcar tracks are seen in the foreground, while the framework for the rooftop terrace is seen above. *AA326.*

By 1924, both the New Battery Park and George Vanderbilt hotels presented competition; in 1926, the Asheville-Biltmore Hotel opened its doors as well. In those years, Asheville was not short on rooms for tourists or conventioneers coming to the mountains. A Langren Hotel postcard of the era advertised "Rooms: single $1.50 to $2.50 Double $2.00 to $4.00."

After World War II, almost everyone had a new automobile, and tourism was no longer just for the rich. An explosion of motor courts and motels dotted the outskirts of town. Tourists weren't as interested in staying downtown as they drove from one vacation spot to another. In the 1950s, the Langren Hotel was leased to the Stiles Hotel Corporation.

By the late 1950s, the Langren, like the once proud Buck Hotel, saw a slow decline in business and began to rent rooms by the week or month.

The Langren's cachet was fading and its business was faltering. New development was planned for the opposite corner of Broadway and College Street. The small parcel of land for "the tallest building in Asheville" needed space for customer parking.

A new parking garage for the new Northwestern Bank Building (later known as the BB&T Building) opened in 1965. It stood on the corner until 2014, when it was razed to make way for another hotel.

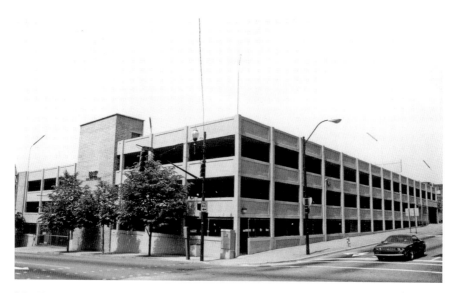

BB&T parking deck, 10 Broadway, at intersection with College Street. Cast-in-place concrete; chain link fence on lower level. Torn down in 2014 and replaced by AC Hotel. *Photograph taken by Rob Neufeld, 1992. MS220.001P.*

The corner of Broadway and College Street has come full circle with the opening of the new AC Hotel Marriott. I've "heard tell" it has a rooftop garden as well.

Chapter 48

THE OTHER DOUGLAS ELLINGTON BUILDINGS ASHEVILLE DIDN'T GET

D ouglas Ellington, born in Clayton, North Carolina, in 1886, was the first southerner to win the coveted Paris Prize in Architecture, the greatest prize awarded in architecture, and the only American at that time to be awarded the Rougevin Prize of the Ecole des Beaux-Arts of Paris, the greatest prize awarded in decorative architecture in Europe.

Ellington first came to Asheville from his office in Pittsburgh, Pennsylvania, in 1925, introducing Art Deco architecture to Asheville with his more traditional design of the First Baptist Church. In 1926, following his contract to design the Asheville City Building, he was named the architect for a proposed plan for the new county building to be erected in connection with the municipal building, then under construction. Many people are familiar with, and bemoan, the decision our county forefathers made not to go with architect Douglas Ellington's proposed twin designs for Asheville City Hall and the Buncombe County Courthouse. His design for the local government buildings came from a desire to have a complex of striking originality and beauty. It is assumed the county commissioners did not find Ellington's design fitting—not quite traditional enough for a county seat—and Ellington's full vision was never realized. In a letter Ellington wrote to the Buncombe County commissioners on January 18, 1927, after he had been notified that he had not been given the contract for the county building, he wrote, "The general scheme as originally contemplated was the only logical solution of the problem possible under the circumstances; and with the buildings and grounds not treated in accordance therewith, then the result will inevitably be nothing more than two separate structures, unrelated, inharmonious, misplaced."

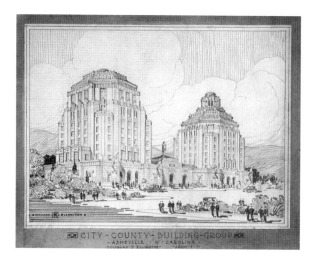

Architect Douglas D. Ellington submitted this architectural sketch for the "city-county-building-group" in 1926. In the design plan, the county courthouse building is a match for the city hall. However, Ellington's vision was thwarted when Buncombe County commissioners awarded the contract to architect Frank Pierce Milburn instead. *M844-8.*

Ellington was then chosen to design the new high school at a site on McDowell Street in January 1927. The design concept was so dramatic that Douglas was honored by Teachers College, Columbia University, for "the best and most beautiful school building of its classification in this country," according to the *Dictionary of North Carolina Biography.* Then on July 10, the *Asheville Citizen* published a "handsome" sketch made by Ellington for a ten-story hotel building to be built on a site on Patton Avenue opposite Ashland Avenue. The construction of the 150- to 180-room hotel, all with baths, to be made of brick, steel and concrete, was expected to begin in six months, according to the unnamed "local and out-of-town capitalists in the project." Apparently, that plan fell through. Oddly enough, NCSU Libraries collection of Ellington drawings also contains a very similar-looking rendering, except it is a sixteen-story building that was to be placed at North Pack Square. The Langren Hotel that faced Broadway is in partial view to the rear left. If a contemporary hotelier or capitalist might like to copy its design, the drawing for it can be found at NCSU Libraries, Rare & Unique Digital Collections.

NCSU Libraries also have an Ellington sketch for a "Recreational Center and Bowling Alleys of Asheville." The one-story building looks much like the Grove Arcade; above the main center doors at the top is a rise with the name "The Alcaza." Alcaza is probably from *alcázar,* a Spanish word derived from Arabic *al-qasr* that refers to a Moorish-type castle or palace.

In November 1928, Ellington was engaged by the S&W Cafeteria to design a three-story building on Patton Avenue. The cafeteria is said to be Ellington's "most refined example of the Art Deco style," according to Clay Griffith's account in "North Carolina Architects & Builders."

As early as 1921, civic officials recognized the need for a new civic center auditorium. In 1937, with funds allotted by the Works Progress Administration, citizens and city officials rose to the occasion to furnish the rest of the funds to replace the previous auditorium that had been abandoned for the past ten years. Addressing community concerns about who was on the committee that decides on the design for the new auditorium, C. Vanderhooven, a city council–appointed auditorium committee member, responded in a letter published in the *Asheville Citizen* on November 10, 1933. He explained that on the previous meeting of Asheville City Council, it appeared that "ethical principles as established in the architects' profession would make it impossible for this group of architects (council had previously asked for the local Architects' Association of Western North Carolina's cooperation and advice) to show their drawings and sketches to the City Council without violating the rules of the American Institute of Architects." However, Asheville architects Lindsey Gudger and Douglas Ellington were independent of the Architects' Association, so they presented their plans. On May 4, 1937, the *Asheville Times* published the architects' drawing of the proposed auditorium as drawn by Lindsey M. Gudger. Ground was broken for the building in February 1938, and the much-anticipated building was dedicated before a crowd of two thousand on January 7, 1940.

And look at what else Asheville didn't get! Ellington also proposed an Art Deco convention hall and auditorium, which is assumed to be the plans Ellington presented to the Asheville City Council. It cannot help but be noticed how Ellington's drawing resembles the current Asheville Civic Center that opened on June 22, 1974, designed by John Cort.

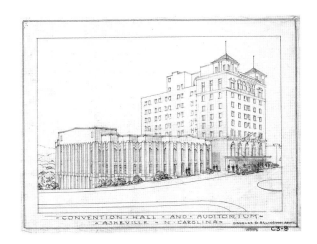

Architect Douglas D. Ellington's proposal for Asheville Convention Hall and Auditorium. The Vanderbilt Hotel is seen at right.*ARD0096.*

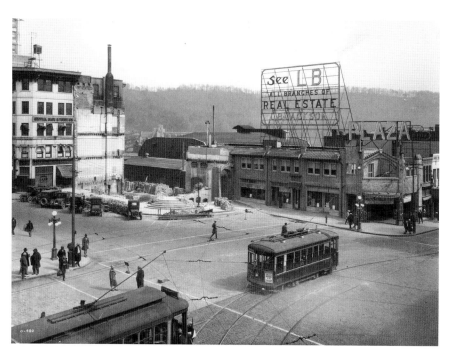

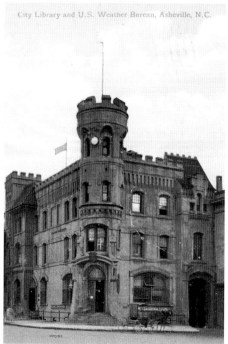

Above: Pack Square South in 1925. The Palmetto building, which housed the old public library, has been demolished to make way for the new library designed by Edward L. Tilton. At left, the Central Bank and Trust sign hangs on the side of the Legal Building. At the Plaza Theater, 6 Biltmore Avenue, Milton Sales and Viola Dana star in *As Man Desires*. The billboard above the Plaza reads: "See LB/ All Branches of/ Real Estate/ L.B. Jackson." Streetcars in the foreground run under a web of wires. The verification of dates for the theater presentation shows that the photo was taken at the end of March 1925. Photo by George Masa. *B145-8M.*

Left: "City Library and weather bureau" in the Palmetto Building (1887, aka First National Bank Building), purchased by George W. Pack in 1897 and then donated to the city for the Asheville Library. The upper floors housed attorneys' offices and the weather bureau from about 1908 until July 1910. The building was demolished 1925. *AA370.*

Chapter 49

WHAT'S NOT IN THIS PHOTOGRAPH?

Being a historian is about learning how to see what is and isn't in a photograph.

This is what's missing! Many people familiar with photographs of Pack Square before the 1920s would recognize this architecturally significant building as Pack Library. Note in the first photo (opposite, top) that the arched entrance seen at the far right and the circular set of stairs at the center entrance are still standing.

For many years before becoming a library, the building had housed the First National Bank. In 1889, the bank purchased and renovated two small brick buildings that predated the Civil War. The two buildings were combined, a castle-like style of architecture was adopted, a third story was added and the exterior was stuccoed. In 1898, the bank went into receivership, and the next year, George W. Pack bought the building and donated it to the city for a library.

The image by Adolph Wittemann on the following page shows the First National Bank in 1887 in all of its spectacular glory just after it had been renovated. This is Buncombe County's sixth courthouse, built in 1875 and replaced in 1903. Note the women with parasols and hooped skirts reminiscent of a Parisian view.

The Asheville Library Association was incorporated on January 25, 1879, and this is the date the library uses to celebrate its birthday. The Asheville Library, originally a subscription library, was in several locations before it found a home in this building for twenty-five years.

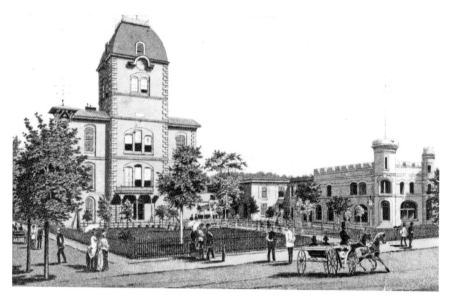

View of Public Square or Court Square, copyrighted 1887 by Adolph Wittemann. *B086-5.*

In January 1919, after forty years as a subscription library, its doors were opened as a free public library, the property having been donated by the Asheville Library Association to the City of Asheville. Free for white citizens of the city who were above the age of twelve, it was officially named Pack Memorial Public Library. Since 1961, all parts of the library system have been opened to all races.

When city officials decided to raze the building, citizens eulogized its history: the building "goes to its doom wrapped with memories of a time that has gone." Being the city's oldest building on the square, it was seen "as the last architectural link between Asheville, the ancient and Asheville, the modern," according to the article "Passing of Old Landmark" in the *Asheville Times* on February 22, 1925.

In 1925, there weren't many people who could exactly remember the history behind the original two buildings, but some recalled that public whippings and the stocks—a means of justice in North Carolina until 1868—took place at the square. Mayor James Eugene Rankin (1846–1928) and Chief of Police W.G. McDowell (1848–1931) recall standing at this site as boys and hearing that a branding was about to take place or having seen offenders put under the lash at the stocks.

J.M. Geary won the bid for razing the Pack Library building, and he began on February 12, 1925. Geary had thirty days to have the site cleared.

City officials were anxious to have the new municipal library designed by architect Edward L. Tilton as a prominent part of their "Program of Progress." Tilton was a prominent New York architect and specialized in the design of libraries. He completed about one hundred in the United States and Canada, including many Carnegie libraries.

On July 9, 1926, the new library opened on the same site as the previous library building on South Pack Square, where it remained for the next fifty years. After a total of seventy-five years on the square, the library moved to its present location at 67 Haywood Street. Designed by Bertram King, the new building was dedicated on November 18, 1978. The year 2019 marks the library's 100th anniversary as a free public library. The old library building on Pack Square now houses the Asheville Art Museum.

Chapter 50

ANTHONY LORD:

ARTIST, ARCHITECT, CRAFTSMAN

Anthony Lord was born in Asheville in 1900, the son of well-known architect William H. Lord and his wife, Helen. After graduating from Yale University in 1927, Anthony Lord spent a year traveling and painting in Europe and then brought home more than seventy sketches in watercolor, ink and pencil, along with hundreds of photographs.

Returning from Europe, Anthony Lord joined his father's firm, which became Lord and Lord, in 1929. During the Depression, he opened Flint Architectural Forgings and produced metalwork for the National Cathedral in Washington, D.C., and for Yale University, as well as for area homes.

In 1933, Lord resumed practicing architecture. In 1941, he helped found Six Associates, a leading southeastern architectural firm. He designed the Asheville Citizen building in 1938, which is still in use by the company today, and was elected to the College of Fellows of the American Institute of Architects in 1957.

Lord also designed the Dillingham Presbyterian Church, D. Hiden Ramsey Library at UNC Asheville and other buildings there and at Warren Wilson College, Western Carolina University and the University of North Carolina at Greensboro. He also designed prominent homes, including the Doan Ogden–John Cram residence in Kenilworth and the Charles D. Owen home in Biltmore Forest, before retiring in 1971.

Seeing urban design as a source of well-being and comfort, Lord was an early advocate of trees in cities, citing a single sycamore tree at the entrance to Wall Street. As early as 1956, he had a letter published in the *Asheville*

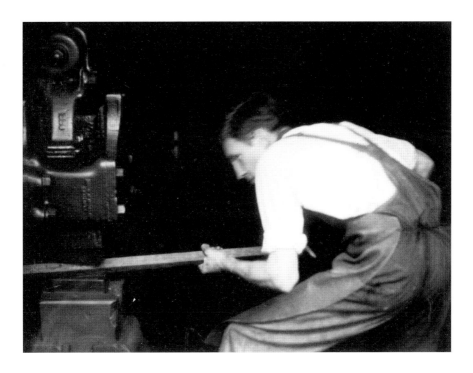

Above: Portrait of Anthony Lord working at Flint Architectural Forgings, 1933. *Taken by Doris Ulmann. L470-5a.*

Right: Anthony Lord ironwork. *Courtesy Peter Austin.*

Citizen stating that if city council would approve replanting trees in the business district, he would give two trees for Pritchard Park.

Talking with anyone who was lucky enough to know "Lord"—as his friends called him—you will learn how impassioned they are about his influence on their lives and how they were empowered by his vast knowledge, character and abilities in many endeavors. Lord loved conversation and sharing wine and good meals and was as interested—if not more so—in the young people

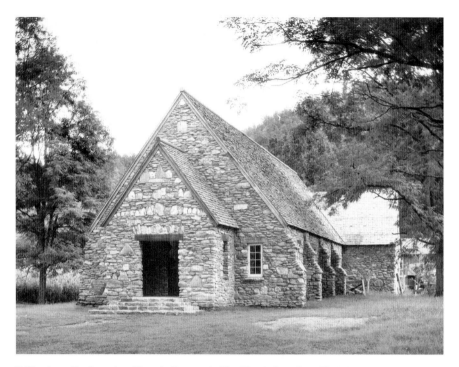

Dillingham Presbyterian Church, Barnardsville, North Carolina. *K767-X*.

around him as in the people who were his own age. John Warner, owner of Warner Photography for over twenty-five years, said that he was most amazed when Lord went out to buy a computer while in his nineties.

Asheville author Elizabeth Johnson Kostova shared what she called the most rewarding experience of her life—working with Lord on the publication of their book, *1927: The Good Natured Chronicle of a Journey*, which was published in 1995. It tells of the trip Lord took to Europe and North Africa in 1927, just after graduating from Yale. The book incorporates photographs, sketches and watercolors that Lord brought home.

Peter Austin, an expert on brick, tile and ironwork, told about how in the 1930s, during the Great Depression, Lord started an ironwork business to make a living. We don't know how much of the ironwork survives in western North Carolina, but we do know that Lord made the gates at the Franklin S. Terry residence in Black Mountain, which later became In-the-Oaks Episcopal Center for the Episcopal Diocese of Western North Carolina. Documenting Lord's wrought ironwork in Asheville still needs to be done; Austin has identified Lord's signature mark—a stylized F-A-F, for the name

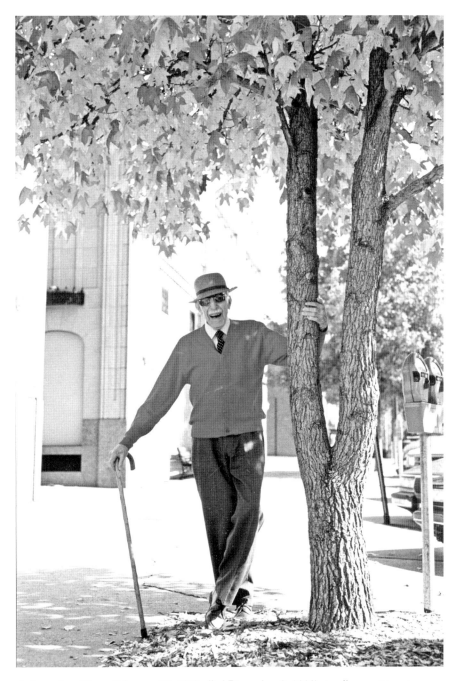

Anthony Lord (born February 17, 1900, died December 9, 1993) standing next to a tree beside the Grove Arcade Building, which had been planted there in his honor and was donated by Roger and Pat McGuire. The photograph was taken by Peggy Gardner on November 1, 1993. *B429-11.*

of his business, Flint Architectural Forgings, which existed circa 1931 to 1937. (The symbol appears more as two curved *E*s meeting over an *A*.)

Artist Dianne Cable, a former lecturer in art for many years at UNC Asheville, appreciates Lord's sketches and watercolors from his 1927 trip to Europe. His early sketches showed his training as an architect and how he was interested in understanding how structures were built. His art evolved over time, giving way imaginatively to a more mature artistic work, allowing the effects of light, color and water—although still controlled—to become the main elements of a painting, with the architectural elements receding.

Asheville photographer Terry Davis sees how photography was yet another art form at which Lord excelled. Apparent in Lord's photographs is his love of architecture, trees in city landscapes, shade, water and people enjoying their surroundings. Viewing them, one can see what was important to the eye of this artist. The Europe photographs make one think about what Lord would bring home within himself and how that would end up affecting his hometown.

Architect John Rogers likes to laughingly say that it seems his lot in life is to defend Lord's architecture. He explains by saying that an architect, for the most part, works for his clients. Rather, Lord's architectural acumen, Rogers says, is exemplified by the buildings at Warren Wilson College and at the grounds of Montreat, Western Carolina University and UNC Greensboro, where his buildings are nestled into the landscape in the midst of trees. Rogers agrees with Lord's approach: "Buildings are shaped by living patterns and by the opportunities nature presents and become an interactive part of the game."

Anthony Lord was many things—an architect, ironworker, community activist, leader of the public library, flutist, lover of nature, watercolor painter, photographer and traveler. He earned the designation Anthony Lord, Renaissance Man. Lord died in Asheville in 1993 at the age of ninety-three. His ashes were scattered on his Flint Street property, with specific care to aid a struggling tomato patch—as he had directed in his will.

EPILOGUE

Every photograph has a story, and the photograph on the following page's story is, in part, about how it got to the North Carolina Room. At first, the notebook-sized cardboard box that arrived in the mail was inconspicuous. But when it was opened at Pack Memorial Library's North Carolina Room, local librarians' jaws started dropping. Inside were the delicate, partly frayed pages of a photo album prepared in 1904, with a handwritten title: "Asheville: The Mountain City in the Land of the Sky, Illustrated." The album contained thirty-four mostly crisp black-and-white pictures that were new to the library's staff.

Whoever prepared the photo album, and for whatever purpose, it took 110 years for it to wend its way to the local library's history collection. And as it happened, the album narrowly escaped the recycling bin of history.

One day in 2013, Lucy Menard, a school librarian in Albany, New York, was perusing "a kind of junk shop" and found a box of mostly local ephemera for sale. Curious, she bought the box for five dollars. Sifting through it, she found Albany-area cards, stationery, playbills and the like, but one nonnative item stood out: a 1904 Asheville photo album. "It sat in my house for at least a year; I'm a bit of a hoarder," Menard said. But one day in the fall of 2014, she set about cleaning and came across the album again.

"I was just about to throw that thing into the recycling," she said. "But then I thought that, even if Asheville already has a copy, maybe they can use another."

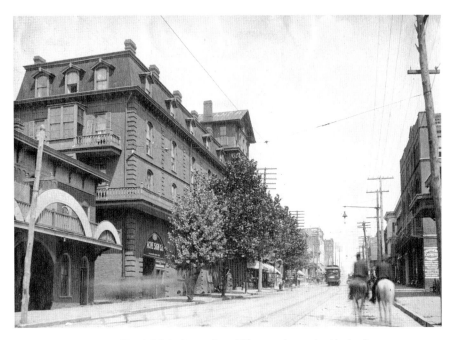

View looking north up North Main Street (later Biltmore Avenue) with the Swannanoa Hotel on the left. *Photographer James McCanless, 1904. MS273 page 006.*

In her surprise package to Pack, Menard added a quick note: "Thought you might want these for the local history archives."

The pictures in the newly discovered album depict Asheville at one of its many historic turning points. As it entered the twentieth century, the town had a population of about 14,600. By 1904, it could boast of having three banks, six schools and twenty churches, along with nine miles of paved roads and fourteen miles of electric streetcar lines. "Asheville is a busy and enterprising city," the 1904 *Asheville City Directory* proclaimed.

Evidence of just how busy and enterprising turns up in the photos, which show everything from classic buildings to public gatherings to everyday street life.

One of our volunteers, Jon Elliston, helped us resurrect this lost piece of history by sharing the story online with Carolina Public Press. Buncombe County multimedia specialist Cataldo Perrone saw Elliston's article about Menard's find and shared it on Buncombe County's Facebook page, where, he said, "it blew up." Then, WLOS TV reporter John Le came by to produce a story for the evening news.

After learning about the splash the photos have made in the North Carolina Collection, Menard said, "It's cool that this turns out to be such a hot find. So many things had to happen along the way for it to finally find a home."

It took quite a long time to figure out who had taken the photographs. We even compared the handwriting to examples we had of photographers' handwriting. In doing so, we discovered that the photographs were taken by James Melton McCanless, an Asheville photographer who kept studios on and near Pack Square from about 1890 to 1920. Surviving examples of his work indicate that he specialized in both intimate portraits and photos of large gatherings and Asheville-area landscapes.

This is the sort of discovery that drives our work, every day, at the North Carolina Room. We're here to receive, sort, explore, investigate and share local history, and while we're grateful to all who helped propel these stories into this book, we await many more. Come see us!

Index

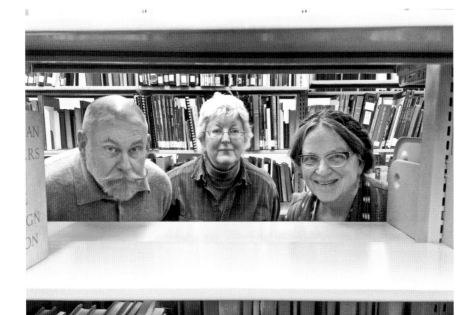

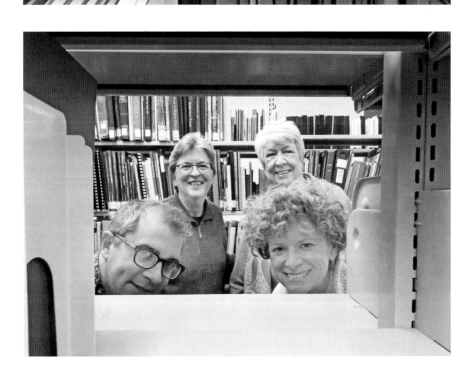

About the North Carolina Room

The North Carolina Room at Pack Memorial Library is dedicated to actively collecting and preserving the history, life and literature of Western North Carolina.

The North Carolina Room has been honored with the following awards:

- The 2013 North Carolina Preservation Consortium Award for Collection Preservation Excellence for its "exemplary collection preservation efforts."
- A 2015 North Carolina State Library Grant of $66,750 to begin digitization of its architectural drawing collection. Library Services and Technology Act (LSTA) funds are awarded by the State Library of North Carolina and made possible through funding from the federal Institute of Museum and Library Services (IMLS) under the provisions of the LSTA as administered by the State Library of North Carolina, a division of the Department of Cultural Resources.
- A 2016 Citizen Architect Award for "preserving and archiving the work of Architects in Asheville and Western North Carolina" by the AIA Asheville Section North Carolina Chapter of the American Institute of Architects.
- A 2017 Award in Education by the Preservation Society of Asheville and Buncombe County for its "highly regarded program series highlighting downtown Asheville in the 1980s."

About the Editor

Z oe Rhine has worked in the North Carolina Room at Pack Memorial Library for more than twenty-five years. She grew up on the Portage Lakes in Akron, Ohio, and the family often visited her mother's relatives in Asheville.

In 1976, she moved to Asheville, where she attended Warren Wilson College, graduating with a bachelor of arts degree in 1980. She received her master of fine arts degree in creative writing from Goddard College in 1989.

She has previously published creative nonfiction stories and taught creative writing courses at the University of North Carolina at Asheville. In 2016, *Mountain Xpress* named her one of Asheville's "Influential Eight" in a quest to find lesser-known folks who were quietly doing important work in the Asheville area.

Visit us at
www.historypress.com
....